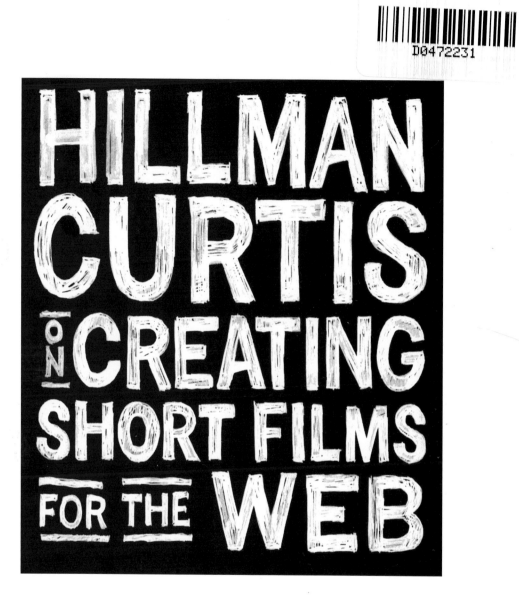

HILLMAN CURTIS ON CREATING SHORT FILMS FOR THE WEB

New Riders

Hillman Curtis on Creating Short Films for the Web
Hillman Curtis

New Riders
1249 Eighth Street
Berkeley, CA 94710
510/524-2178
800/283-9444
510/524-2221 (fax)
Find us on the Web at www.peachpit.com.
To report errors, please send a note to errata@peachpit.com
New Riders is an imprint of Peachpit, a division of Pearson Education.

Editor: Ted Waitt
Senior Executive Editor: Marjorie Baer
Production Editor: Hilal Sala
Interior Design: Charlene Will
Compositor: Kim Scott
Indexer: Ken DellaPenta
Proofreader: Evan Pricco
Appendix Tech Edit: Robert Reinhardt
Cover Design/Hand Lettering: Fran Gaitanaros/The Rooster Design Group
Cover Photograph: Matthias Ernstberger

ISBN 0-321-27891-7

9 8 7 6 5 4 3 2 1

Printed and bound in the United States of America

This book is dedicated to the late Paul Allen Zimmerman.

I'd also like to thank the following people:

My wife, Christina, whom I rely on to either approve or veto whatever I do, and my son, Jasper.

David Alm for all of his hard work making this book happen—it wouldn't have happened without his expert writing and editing.

My editor, Ted Waitt, who was a valued collaborator and editor and who went far beyond the call of duty to make sure the book got done.

Ben Wolf for sharing his passion for film and for making sure digital video filmmaking was explained properly.

My intern, David Chang, who prepared and processed all of the book's images.

My acquiring editor, Marjorie Baer, who put up with the many different incarnations of the book.

Charlene Will and Kim Scott designed a beautiful interior, Hilal Sala made sure the book got to the printer on time, Fran Gaitanaros designed the cover, Matthias Ernstberger took the cover photo, Jens Loeffler wrote the appendix, Robert Reinhardt tech edited it, and Joe Lowery helped me get started. To all...thanks.

TABLE OF CONTENTS

Introduction, 2

Getting Started, 10

The Visitors: Messengers and a New Camera, 26

Falling in Love with Movement, 54

60 Seconds with...Sum 41, 70

My Favorite Designers, 88

Nonlinear Storytelling, 118

Striking Out as a Music Video Director, 142

Making a Movie, 166

Conclusion, 192

Appendix: Why Flash Video?, 208

Contributors, 222

Credits, 224

Index, 226

INTRODUCTION

Where's My Camera?

It's late on a winter night, and I'm sitting alone in a corner bistro in Chelsea. There are huge windows looking out onto Ninth Avenue. Taxis and cars flash by, all color and lights. Across from me a single woman eats alone, and to my right, the lone waiter sits with a book. The lighting in here couldn't be better, my espresso-addled mind is reaching for an imaginary DV camera, and I'm off daydreaming again. I'm dreaming of the shots I could get here, of capturing the perfect light that is falling on the woman's face. The light is so good that I'm even thinking about coming back tomorrow night with my DV camera and tripod, and asking the most interesting person I see if I can shoot them, portrait style.

Digital video, affordable cameras, FireWire, and amazing desktop editing software are the first creative tools to come along in years that make my heart beat faster. The idea of possibly making a fool of myself in public for something as fleeting as the light on a beautiful woman's face is exciting to me. For a creative person, there's nothing like realizing that you can still surprise yourself, and when you do you want to tell the world...or at least I do.

Which is why I'm in this café writing. I believe that DV represents the future for rich media online—just as I believed in the future of Flash back in the mid-1990s. As bandwidth continues to increase and compression utilities become more efficient, more and more companies will turn to DV on the Web to set their messages apart from the competition, much as they did six years ago with Flash.

Why Digital Video?

Situations like the one in the café are happening more and more. I'm starting to make some changes, and I know I'm not alone. I've been a Web designer for the last eight or nine years. It's how I make a living, and it's where the change is happening. Since 2002, when I put up a series of video portraits on my company's homepage, I've been fielding calls from people asking how they might use digital video online as a way to tell a story about their company, products, or themselves.

In the not-so-distant past you had to go to film school to learn filmmaking—and to get your hands on some gear. Film school is still a great resource for those who can afford it, but for those of us too old or too poor or too entrenched in our careers to enroll, digital video is the answer. With every film I shoot and edit, I make an embarrassing number of mistakes. I choose the wrong location, screw up the sound, or over/underlight the scene. They're painful mistakes, but I learn from them and I get better.

The setup could hardly be simpler. I own one very good three-chip camera, one shotgun mic, one tripod, and two halogen lights. I can—and do—travel to shoots on my bicycle, gear loaded up, through the streets of Manhattan. I rarely use assistants and, with about $1,000 worth of software, I edit on a laptop—on airplanes, at cafés, and at my kitchen table. And I learn as I go.

My Background

I've been immersed in the digital design world since the mid-1990s, when I was the Art Director at Macromedia (now Adobe). During that time the firm developed Flash and asked me to explore its capabilities even before it hit the streets. I loved Flash from the start. It offered me the opportunity to work with motion, and to tell stories in a time-based medium. It also gave me the chance to experiment with rhythm and pacing, and I started to become aware of how the eye follows motion.

In 1998 I moved to New York, founded my own company, and began experimenting with digital video to capture sequential images for my Flash movies. Through this I was able to create little moments that resembled film motion, but my passion wasn't satisfied. I started imagining larger projects, hoping I could eventually do some bona fide filmmaking. In the years since, digital video has become a primary focus for me—no longer a tool servicing another application, like Flash. In short, New Media has once again allowed me to reinvent myself.

I'm still very much a designer, but I've become a filmmaker as well, though not in the traditional sense, as I shoot my films digitally and stream them on the Web. I feel different from the New Media designer I was when I wrote my last book, *MTIV: Process, Inspiration and Practice for the New Media Designer*, in 2002. I've even begun introducing myself as a designer *and* a filmmaker at social gatherings, and it feels good—like a promise.

In this book I describe nine of my DV projects: what they were, what inspired them, and how I did them. You can see almost all of these films on my company's Web site, hillmancurtis.com. Each project contains certain principles of filmmaking—many of which were conceived decades ago—and I use those principles to illuminate my own process. Then I describe in detail how I went about executing each project through trial-and-error, and offer my experience on what worked and what didn't. I hope these sections will help you avoid the pitfalls I found along the way, though I also recognize that mistakes are often crucial to the creative process. My hope, then, is less to instruct than to inspire—to help you make the best films you can.

GETTING STARTED

PERHAPS IT SOUNDS RIDICULOUS,

BUT THE BEST THING THAT YOUNG

FILMMAKERS SHOULD DO IS

TO GET HOLD OF A CAMERA AND

SOME FILM AND MAKE A MOVIE

OF ANY KIND AT ALL.

—STANLEY KUBRICK

Years ago the technical aspects of filmmaking were a real barrier for me. I knew nothing about cameras, film stock, lighting, sound, or editing systems—which at that time were mainly expensive Avid systems. Worse, I felt I had no way to learn. Everything was expensive: the film stock, the cameras, etc. And when it came to editing, you had to hire an editor and rent an editing suite. I'm a DIY (Do It Yourself) type. I prefer to retreat to a corner somewhere and make mistakes in private, and that didn't seem possible with filmmaking in the past. It always seemed I'd need some sort of crew. So when digital video and DV editing software came onto my horizon, I didn't hesitate. I could rent or buy a camera, buy the editing software, and begin. And I could do it myself.

This is an exciting time to explore digital filmmaking. Digital cameras are good and getting better. The same camera that director Danny Boyle used for his 2002 movie, *28 Days Later*, is available for just a few thousand dollars (he used Canon XL1s for the film, manned by Anthony Dod Mantle, who may be the best DV cinematographer in the business). A single MiniDV tape, our "film stock," costs less than 10 dollars and requires none of the expensive processing that film does. Editing software and the necessary computers are both reasonably priced as well, and the software is intuitive and easy to learn.

That said, there are a few things that are helpful to know.

EQUIPMENT

The list of basic equipment you need is pretty concise: a camera, a tripod, and a computer which runs an editing application. A decent microphone and headphones are also helpful.

Cameras

Digital video cameras may not be dirt cheap (yet) but they are certainly affordable. The key is making sure that whatever camera you buy has a FireWire port. Known as i.LINK on Sony models and IEEE 1394 generically, FireWire allows you to transfer footage from your MiniDV tape in the camera directly to the computer's hard drive.

Digital video cameras fall into two primary categories: one- and three-chip. One-chip cameras are smaller, consumer-oriented products that use a single CCD (Charge Coupled Device) chip to process all the color information received by the lens. Three-chip cameras dedicate a different CCD chip to each primary color: red, green, and blue. Either type of camera is fine, but three-chip cameras offer higher quality.

Right now, I use a Panasonic DVX100, a three-chip camera best described as a miniature pro camera. It has external manual controls for every function—zoom, focus, iris, shutter speed, gain, ND filters, white balance, and audio levels. These manual controls are the main components of what qualifies it as a "serious" or "professional" camera. Additionally it has a wonderful Leica lens and built-in audio inputs adaptable to professional audio gear. Finally, it has a wide variety of menu functions that allows you to have ultimate control over your shots.

Learning to use your camera's manual controls is vital to really getting the most out of your shoot. Here's a quick rundown of the basics.

Zoom Most people have an intuitive grasp of what the zoom control does, but there's more to it than just telescoping in and out. The focal length of a lens determines whether the environment around the subject is in focus or not—wide lenses show the world, while long lenses show only a very small arc of it. Focal length is also the primary means of controlling depth of field; with a wide lens, everything will be in focus, while a telephoto lens will yield a shallow depth of field, enabling the shooter to throw a background out of focus.

Focus Learn to focus your camera manually! When autofocus works perfectly (and it rarely does), it focuses on whatever is dead center in the frame. But what if the subject of your shot is off center? To focus manually, zoom all the way in on the subject, focus, and then pull back to your desired framing.

Iris Iris is the first of four ways to adjust exposure—the brightness of the image. Exposure is critical in video, because video tape has a very limited margin for error. If exposure is even slightly off, the image can either "blow out" or get lost in darkness. The iris is analogous to the eye's pupil—the larger the diameter (the smaller the F-stop), the more light reaches the CCD chip(s). The iris control also affects depth of field—in fact, on any camera, there are only two controls that can alter DOF: zoom (mentioned above) and iris. The wider your camera's iris, the shallower your depth of field.

Shutter The second control that affects exposure, shutter speed, refers to the amount of time each frame of video is exposed to the light. The shorter the exposure, the darker the image. Standard shutter speed for normal video is 1/60 second (or 60 frames per second), and for 24P video it's 1/48 second. Besides affecting exposure, the shutter speed also alters the motion quality of the video. A slow shutter will result in a streaky image, while a fast shutter will result in a strobe effect (think *Saving Private Ryan*). Because of these motion issues, shutter speed is usually only manipulated to achieve a special effect.

Gain The third control affecting exposure, gain, is analogous to the volume control on a stereo. If an audio tape is recorded too low, you can always crank up the volume—but the result will be a lot of hiss. Similarly, the gain (measured in decibels) electronically boosts the signal coming off the CCD chip(s), enabling the shooter to work in very low-light conditions—but the image quality will suffer. So gain is generally used only as a last resort, when better lighting options are exhausted or unavailable.

ND filters The last of the four exposure-affecting controls, ND (Neutral Density) filters, are like sunglasses for your camera. Most "prosumer" cameras have one or two grades of ND filters built in, which can be employed with the flip of a switch. Any camera can also accommodate screw-on ND filters, which can be purchased at any professional camera store. For some mysterious reason, an ND3 filter darkens the image one F-stop, an ND6 two F-stops, etc. Unlike the other three controls affecting exposure, ND filters have no "side effects"—they simply darken the image.

White balance Even to our eyes, daylight (scientifically described as 5600 degrees Kelvin) is bluer, or "cooler," than the light from a light bulb (3200 degrees Kelvin). Video cameras tend to exaggerate this difference, so for colors to appear natural (particularly skin tones), we have to tell the camera what sort of light is illuminating the subject. White balance can be set to a camera's built-in daylight or tungsten preset, or can be set manually. To set white balance manually, place a sheet of white paper in the position of the subject, fill the camera's frame with the sheet of paper, and activate the manual white balance function.

Audio levels Professional cameras offer manual control of the microphone's audio levels, which are the equivalent of exposure for sound. Essentially, the camera can't handle the same range of volume as the human ear. So, in conjunction with audio level meters, the camera must be set to pick up quiet sounds (in which case loud sounds will distort) or loud sounds (in which case quiet sounds will barely be recorded).

Microphones

It's easy to get lost in the beauty of a shot, but remember that a beautiful shot of a person speaking is worthless if you can't make out what he or she is saying. Having good mics can really elevate a project. I own a Sennheiser ME66/K shotgun mic, which cost about $500, and I use it on almost every shoot. It's a uni-directional mic that can be mounted on the camera or on a boom. Here's a quick rundown on mics.

Directional shotgun mic The most versatile and generally best sounding type of mic. A shotgun mic favors sounds coming from the direction in which it's pointing (uni-directional). This makes the shotgun mic ideal for use in environments with unwanted ambient sound—but also requires that the mic be pointed directly at the subject. As no mic works well beyond three or four feet from the subject, a shotgun mic is typically placed in an isolating shockmount at the end of a boompole (also called a "fishpole"), which is held over the speaker's head, just above the frameline. Since shotguns are very sensitive, they must be protected from the wind when outdoors, typically with a furry windscreen (also known as a "softie").

Lavalier mic The small clip-on mic that is typically attached directly to a subject's shirt or coat. The advantage of this mic over the shotgun is that no boom operator is required and, when necessary, the mic can be hidden under clothing. Disadvantages include a less natural sound, the constant annoyance of clothes rustling, and the cable that connects the subject to the camera. Of course, a wireless transmitter/receiver device can be used—and these are great when they work well—but they're expensive and susceptible to radio interference.

Built-in camera mic   As a rule, this is the last resort for a couple of reasons. First, built-in mics are generally low-quality, omni-directional mics, picking up nearly as much sound from behind the camera as in front of it. Moreover, since mics only work well when they're in close proximity to a subject, you can't position your camera more than a few feet from your subject when using a built-in mic.

Speakers and Headphones

A good set of speakers and headphones are a worthwhile invest-ment as well. They allow you to monitor, process, and correct audio, both in the field and in the editing suite.

Computers and Software

I do all my video editing and Web work on a Macintosh. I use the current version of Final Cut Pro and I cut on a G4 laptop running at 1.5 GHz with 1 gig of memory. You can run Final Cut on a less sophisticated machine, of course.

Other programs include Avid, which makes a full range of edit-ing software for both Mac and Windows. Adobe's Premiere Pro is also a solid program. It stacks up well against Final Cut Pro, it's cheaper, and it offers excellent integration with other Adobe programs, such as Photoshop and After Effects. At the time of this writing, Adobe Premiere Pro is a PC-only product. Sony also offers a PC-friendly program called Vegas Video.

External FireWire Drive

Although an external FireWire drive is optional, I can't recommend it highly enough. Hard drive prices have dropped considerably over the years, to the point of making them almost disposable. In fact, I budget a drive into every project I take on, and when the project wraps I stash the drive on a shelf and hope to never have to use it again. But I know the project is on it and ready to access, should a client call requesting a quick change or update. When shopping for a drive, keep in mind the basic formula: 15 gigs per hour of DV footage. You should also look for drives rated to spin at 7200 RPM and have a data-transfer rate of about 7 to 8 MB per second.

MiniDV Deck

A MiniDV deck is basically a convenience. Typically, your MiniDV deck maintains a constant FireWire connection to your Mac—you just have to take the tape out of your camera and place it in your MiniDV deck. While you can transfer your digital video directly from the FireWire port on your camera to your computer, a MiniDV deck frees up your camera for continued use. It also sidesteps the hassle of continually connecting and disconnecting the FireWire cable. Final Cut Pro will recognize the deck when the program launches and you'll be ready to capture your recorded video footage.

NTSC Monitor

I began using an NTSC monitor because I was getting requests to record my Web projects to DVDs. Because video looks very different on a TV than on a computer monitor, an NTSC monitor—or PAL in some regions—will help you color and frame your video correctly for a TV screen. In many cases, you may opt to create two versions of your project: one for a purely digital environment, like the Web, and another for the analog, NTSC-driven realm.

PROCESS

The path I take from start to finish is pretty direct: shoot the footage, capture and edit the footage in Final Cut Pro, compress my final cut for online playback, and upload the spot to the Web.

Pre-Production

Pre-production consists of all the planning that takes place before the shoot begins—including writing a script, choosing a location, securing talent and crew, renting gear, coming up with a shot plan, and rehearsing. Some rigorously controlled styles rely heavily on pre-production. My approach tends to be more spontaneous and improvisational, and is thus light on pre-production. (As I'll discuss later, however, this can be as much a liability as an asset.)

Production

Production refers to the shoot itself, those days when the camera is actually rolling. I've found every shooting experience to be unique, and this book focuses on different projects to convey how varied the production process can be.

Log and Capture

Logging and capturing is where you organize and transfer the digital data from your MiniDV tape to your computer's hard drive. You connect your camera or MiniDV deck to your computer with a FireWire cable and, using the capturing feature in a digital-editing program, capture your footage. Although many people dread the log-and-capture process, considering it boring and mechanical, I've come to appreciate it as an essential part of the editing process.

There are two sides to logging and capturing—one creative, the other technical. Logging is creative because it allows the filmmaker to really learn his or her footage and make those first critical decisions about what to keep and what to throw out. Often, initial intentions must be thrown out, as the footage needs to be viewed with a fresh pair of eyes. Maybe some moments in the shoot didn't work out—but new and unforeseen things happened, too. The filmmaker is asking him- or herself how this material can be used to make the best possible film.

On the technical side, the logging process allows the editor to create an organizational structure that will best facilitate the edit. Clips should be given meaningful—i.e., memorable and appropriate—titles, and then placed in folders that will make them easy to sort and locate throughout the post-production process.

Editing (Post)

The edit is where you assemble the different shots from your production. It's also where you build a soundtrack, color correct your footage, and add visual effects, titles, and transitions—like dissolves or fades.

I think I might be more of an editor than a director or cinematographer—at least at the time of this writing—and I'm a huge fan of the editing process in general. To me this is where the project really takes shape. Certainly in my documentary work, the edit is where I find the story.

Editing, or "post," is just as creatively significant as the actual shoot or production process. The great director Stanley Kubrick once said that he considered the production phase to be simply a prelude to the edit.

Compression

Video is file-size heavy, and to make it a viable Web medium you have to compress it. Compression essentially squeezes data into a smaller file so it can effectively pass through the Web's limited bandwidths. That data is then decompressed and played back on the receiving end through a player, such as QuickTime Player, Windows Media Player, Flash, or RealPlayer. These players are technically "codecs," which is short for compression/decompression. I've heard this process described as analogous to sending and receiving a letter: first you fold it to fit in an envelope so you can send it, then the recipient unfolds the letter to read it.

Most editing software comes with a compression utility. In the case of Final Cut Pro, Apple dug deep and came up with a creative title for its utility: "Compressor." This utility offers the user compression presets, as well as the ability to dial in your own settings. There are also a number of third-party compression utilities, such as Sorenson Squeeze and Media Cleaner Pro.

Why I Use Flash Video

Until fairly recently, viewing Web video required that you have one of the three big players: QuickTime, RealOne, or Windows Media Player. Consequently, when displaying video on the Web, a typical strategy was to offer the same video in multiple formats. That situation has changed rapidly since Macromedia introduced Flash video in 2003.

Macromedia Flash is known for its eye-popping animations, sophisticated navigation, and rich Internet applications. With the release of Flash MX, video was added to the mix. Flash video uses a similar codec as QuickTime, and its display output can be of a very high quality. But unlike other players, the Flash Player is ubiquitous: it's available cross-platform and cross-browser on over 95% of current computer systems—and that statistic is for Flash Player 6, the first video-capable version. It's only bound to get better.

Another benefit to using Flash video is the incredible interactivity it offers. Because Flash video is embedded in a Flash movie, the sky's the limit when it comes to integrating designer control and user interaction. Everything you can do in a Flash movie, you can do with Flash video. For example, you could create a marketing campaign where the soundtrack playing behind the product is also for sale, and allow the viewer to download and buy the music while the video is streaming.

With QuickTime, RealOne, or Windows Media Player, you launch a movie and it loads in a pop-up window, separate from the Web page you were viewing. With Flash, though, you get an immediate, "in-page" experience. That is, when you open a Web page that features a properly structured Flash video, you see the video immediately and it's ready to play—in fact, it may already be playing. The first of my own projects that I deconstruct in this book, The Visitors portrait series, appears so quickly, and the subject is so stationary, that many people initially mistake the image for a static JPEG—until the subject blinks.

In Sum

It's important to stay current and take advantage of the latest developments in digital video, but only to the extent that they don't overwhelm or intimidate you. The thing I try to remember is that my primary challenge is to tell a story or convey a theme, and I know I can do that with a simple portrait as well as with something more technically complex. I also remind myself that movies like *28 Days Later* and *Celebration*, both shot on prosumer DV cameras and produced with relatively small budgets, are far more compelling than many giant-budget Hollywood movies that feature the latest in special effects and technology.

The point is not whether you take big or small steps...but to take the step that allows you to express yourself. In doing that, you will discover the technology as you need it. At least this is how I've been doing it. I hope this primer helps.

THE VISITORS :
MESSENGERS AND A NEW CAMERA

MY PORTRAITS ARE MORE
ABOUT ME THAN THEY
ARE ABOUT THE PEOPLE
I PHOTOGRAPH.

—RICHARD AVEDON

I've been shooting video portraits for almost two years now. I have close to 60 individual portraits at this point and I still enjoy shooting them. I started this series because I wanted to learn how to work a new video camera. But that was only part of it. The series was also a deliberate attempt to balance my life, to reconnect myself with art. I started the series at the tail end of some bad years. Years that saw the apparent loss of democracy (in the 2000 election), the threat of terrorism made real on 9/11, and a serious downturn in our economy.

During those years it felt like a dark cloud floating above our nation and certainly above parts of the world, and I dealt with it by doing what I always do...losing myself in my work. I put blinders on and stared at the computer. I took an endless series of jobs that, given the economic climate, I was lucky to have, but they were—for the most part—repetitive and neither engaging nor particularly challenging. And what happened was that I simply disengaged. I started hiding from the world and as an artist that is the kiss of death. I think it is the job of an artist to engage with, and then react and respond to the world...both the good and the bad.

My decision to shoot portraits—and even to allow myself to buy a new, expensive camera—was the result of a string of events that, one by one, started to wake me up.

In the summer of 2002, I was invited to give a talk at Expression College for Digital Arts, a New Media school in Oakland. In the audience that night was an old friend from my punk rock days. Jimmy had been a DJ while I was a bartender at a nightclub in San Francisco called Nightbreak. We hung out for three or four years—maybe '83 to '87—working at the club, wearing Doc Martens, poodle haircuts, leather jackets, and the occasional dress. So there he was, 15-odd years later, working, I found out, as an instructor at the school.

After I finished my talk, a bunch of us went for dinner and drinks. Jimmy and I sat next to each other and spent the night catching up. He told me about the road he took that led him to where he was, and I told him about mine. Weeks later I got an email from him.

Hey H,

It was great seeing you. But for me, around the beginning of this year, things were going so bad, I was losin' it. I realize now, I was losing hope. The word HOPE has been a big theme for me lately. The possibility that something good might happen is the fuel. I think you said Joy is the engine. I think Hope is the fuel. Anyway, the past week or so, it came back. It just took a couple of things to happen, and a couple of hours spent creating music again and voila, I gots me some hope back. Then, you do your speech and it was right on track with what I'd been feeling. I'm just telling you all this cuz I was so high on wine that night I never got to tell you how much I liked your speech.

All the best
xoxoxoxox
Jimmy

I showed Jimmy's note to my wife, which prompted her to talk about her belief in messages and messengers. She explained that when I gave my talk—the theme of which was hope, specifically nurturing the hope that what you do can have an impact on the world—I was a messenger to Jimmy. Now, with his note, he was returning the favor, presenting a message to me. And as it turns out, the message was the same: hope. Jimmy reminded me that with art we have the opportunity—indeed, the responsibility—to engage with, react to, and, ideally, influence the world.

With that I decided to open myself up for messages, which is to say I started to seek them out. And the messages—it's as if you are telling yourself what you already know, or connecting with your God or your true purpose, your guiding light or angel, your inner voice—started to reveal themselves. It's not magic, the messages are always there. But by opening yourself up, you start to really notice them.

I used to pass a gym on my way to work that had a huge glass window revealing the various workout areas inside. One was a boxing area, with a mini ring, bags, and a speed bag. In my early twenties, I had done a little boxing at an old-school gym in San Francisco's Tenderloin neighborhood, so out of nostalgia I'd sometimes slow my pace to check out the guys hitting the bag or sparring.

I was feeling old and tired, and one morning I decided I'd get back in shape. So I joined the gym. One of the things I got when I joined was a free session with a trainer. I showed up for my lesson with my old gloves and I was bouncing around like a fool, jabbing at the bag, when my trainer came up. He said that he could tell I'd boxed before, which made me feel good, but told me I had a couple of fundamentals wrong.

"First," he said, "you're all crouched over, all covered up. You have to use your God-given gifts. You're tall. Stand up straight." So I did. "You're also facing the bag sideways. Square off on your opponent; otherwise, you can't throw the right."

This was a pretty standard boxing lesson. But that morning I took more from it. The trainer unwittingly relayed messages that I needed to hear. First, to stop covering up, and stop hiding from the world. Second, to acknowledge my blessings, stand up straight, and face my opponents. This could be anything: a client situation, a creative challenge, or a career shift—all of which I was facing at that time. And finally, and most important, to "throw the right." The right is the knockout punch, but by throwing it you leave yourself vulnerable to getting hit, perhaps even knocked out, yourself. But you have to throw it to win—even to compete.

Around that time I came upon a short interview with one of my favorite artists, Robert Rauschenberg, in *Time Out New York*, a weekly urban lifestyle magazine. I tore out one of the questions and pasted it in my notebook for future inspiration.

It's the same message Jimmy and I passed back and forth, and that my boxing trainer imparted: you can make a difference; you just have to try.

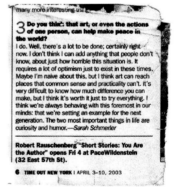

many more interesting that

3 **Do you think that art, or even the actions of one person, can help make peace in the world?**
I do. Well, there's a lot to be done; certainly right now. I don't think I can add anything that people don't know, about just how horrible this situation is. It requires a lot of optimism just to exist in these times. Maybe I'm naïve about this, but I think art can reach places that common sense and practicality can't. It's very difficult to know how much difference you can make, but I think it's worth it just to try everything. I think we're always behaving with this foremost in our minds: that we're setting an example for the next generation. The two most important things in life are curiosity and humor.—*Sarah Schmerler*

Robert Rauschenberg "Short Stories: You Are the Author" opens Fri 4 at PaceWildenstein (32 East 57th St).

6 TIME OUT NEW YORK | APRIL 3–10, 2003

That fall I also received a gift from Bill Viola, one of the most prolific and innovative video artists working today. It was a signed copy of his latest book, *Bill Viola: The Passions*. I opened the book and read the inscription he had written: "For Hillman, Aim high! Keep moving!" Beside the inscription he drew a monitor with an arrow flying out of it. The message was clear.

I mentioned earlier that I was losing myself in a series of jobs, coasting through the months, neither aiming high nor moving forward. Worse yet, I was looking at the computer as a paycheck and not as the amazing, creative tool it is. To me, Bill's message said, "Redefine your relationship with this tool, look outside that tiny monitor. Shoot for the stars, or at least look up to the sky once in awhile."

It took a couple of days for the message to set me in motion, but when it did I went out and bought the DV camera I'd been wanting for months: the Panasonic DVX100. The Visitors portrait series followed shortly thereafter. It was my first non-client project in three years.

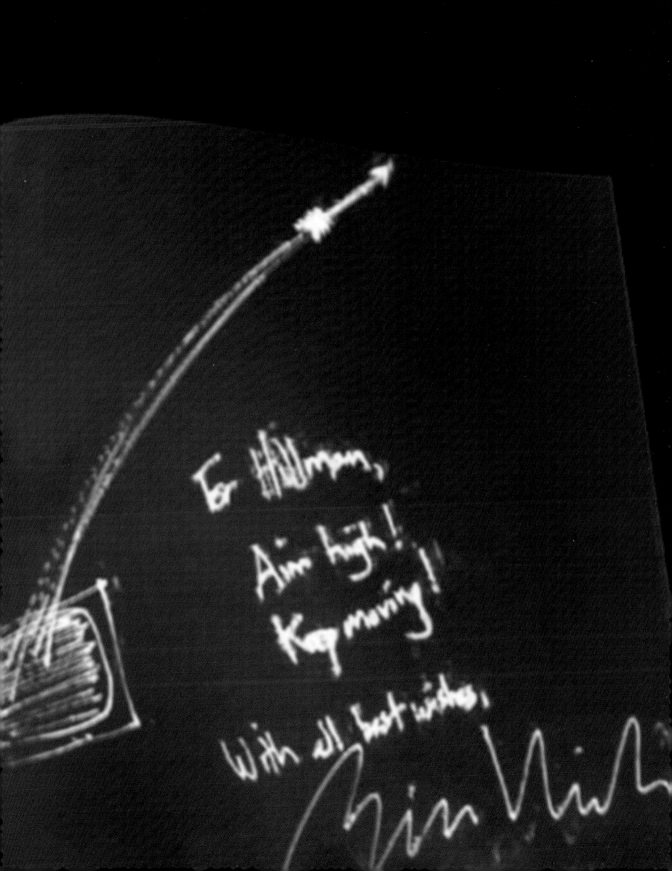

The Concept

The Panasonic DVX100 is a wonderful camera, capable of capturing beautiful footage, but it's also quite a bit more complicated than my previous camera. I needed a project that would help me learn how to use it, but I also wanted this project to be for myself. I didn't want the constraints or worries that so often accompany a client job.

Looking for inspiration, I turned to Viola's book. I fell in love—or re-fell in love—with some of the stills from his work *Observance* from 2002. Gorgeously framed and lit, caught by moments of intense emotion, the figures in Viola's stills got me thinking about capturing a person's essence on video.

Then I remembered the work of Thomas Ruff, a German photographer whose portrait series grabbed me one day as I leafed through a copy of *Art and Photography* (Phaidon Press, edited by David Campany). Ruff began his ongoing portrait series in 1986 and uses various colored backgrounds to frame his subjects in reds, light blues, whites, blacks, and yellows. I was taken with the careful framing of each subject in his portraits. The colors are perfect, with skin tones slightly desaturated and blown out, and the backdrops work to accentuate the subject's hair color, clothes, and skin tone.

Finally, I remembered the brilliant film work of the late documentary filmmaker Jean Rouch. A major influence on the French New Wave directors of the early 1960s, such as Jean-Luc Godard and Francois Truffaut, Rouch coined the term *cinema verité*—literally "film truth"—and, like Viola, he sought to capture his subjects' *inner* realities—their psyches and emotions—on film.

In his 1961 documentary *Chronicle of a Summer*, Rouch interviews four Parisians, beginning each interview with a single question: *Are you happy?* Once they begin to answer, he holds the camera on them until well after their guards are down, making themselves utterly vulnerable to the camera's eye. The results are breathtaking. Over the course of the 85-minute film Rouch creates an elliptical narrative structure that always brings us back to the same subjects, revealing their personalities gradually and in concert with one another. Two men and two women—a student, a factory worker, a Holocaust survivor, and a receptionist—open themselves completely to Rouch and, consequently, to us, the viewers. The camera becomes not just a recording device, but also a tool, essentially turning the subjects inside out.

Each of these artists—Viola, Ruff, and Rouch—managed to do precisely what I wanted to try myself: capture a person's essence on film or video.

So I set up a colored background, much like Ruff's, but like Viola and Rouch, shot moving instead of still images. Before this project, I'd always approached a video shoot rather haphazardly—I'd point, shoot, and fix the footage later in the edit. But this project forced me to think more carefully about what I was shooting. Because the shots would be so simple—just one per subject—the lighting, framing, and focus had to be perfect.

I get a lot of visitors to my studio: mostly clients, friends, and design students on class trips. So I decided to use this constant supply of visitors as my subjects—hence the name of this project: The Visitors.

The Shoot

I've shot the series in four places so far: my home in Grass Valley, California; a temporary studio in San Francisco; my apartment in New York; and my primary studio, also in New York. In each setting, the shoots were all pretty spartan, requiring just a tripod, camera, and backdrop—a thick piece of colored construction paper tacked to the wall. I used a low-backed chair and positioned it in front of the backdrop.

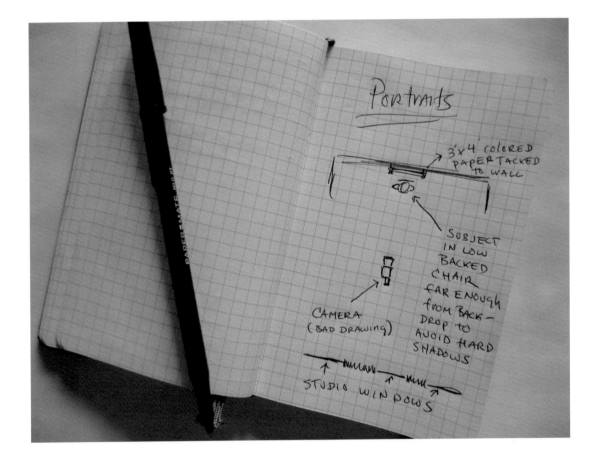

My first inclination was to use two Tota (halogen) lights, directly to the left and right of my tripod. I shot the first five or six portraits this way, but I wasn't happy with the results, as hard shadows were appearing around the subjects' noses and eyes. The light from the Totas was too hard.

As I learned more about lighting, I came to appreciate that lights have four characteristics, and that each of these characteristics can be controlled in order to truly "paint with light."

- **Brightness or intensity**—the subject must be appropriately illuminated, but not "blown out."

- **Direction**—where is the light coming from? People tend to look best and most three dimensional when the main or "key" source of lighting is placed about 45 degrees from an imaginary line between the camera and subject. But sometimes sidelighting or even backlighting a subject is the key to achieving a desired effect.

- **Color**—colored plastic gels can be used to change the hue of a light. Subjects can be "warmed up" to give them a healthy glow, or "cooled down" with tungsten lights to match daylight. The possibilities are unlimited.

- **Quality**—this is the area of lighting least appreciated by the layman, and refers to how hard or soft a light is. Hard lights cast hard shadows, while soft lights gently "wrap" around the illuminated subject. Soft lighting is one of the keys to achieving lighting that flatters your subject. What makes a light soft is its size—in short, the bigger the source, the softer the light. So a small (and by definition hard) film light can be made into a soft light by bouncing it off a large reflector or shooting it through a large piece of diffusing fabric.

During the project's early stages I came upon an interview with the great cinematographer Sven Nykvist, who directed the photography for most of Ingmar Bergman's films. He said he'd lucked into the job after Bergman's first cinematographer had quit a project early on, and described the first shot he had to do: an interior scene at night. He was nervous, this being his first job as a DP and the first time he'd worked with such a famous director, so he went all-out, setting numerous lights to create an intense, dramatic look.

The shoot went fine, but when Bergman saw the dailies the following day, he flipped, yelling, "How the hell do you have hard shadows at night?!"

Nykvist had overlit the shot and the scene appeared unnatural. From that point on, he and Bergman pursued natural light whenever possible. He explained that they'd scout a location for several days before beginning a shoot, taking notes on how the light changed over the course of a single day, and under various weather conditions. Nykvist went on to become a master cinematographer, helping to establish Bergman's reputation as one of the world's pre-eminent filmmakers.

So I took a lesson from Nykvist. I dismantled my lights, moved my backdrop and tripod closer to the window, and shot a few more portraits. The result was much richer than the previous attempts, with subtle fluctuations in the light on my subjects' faces, creating an almost filmic look. Some even began looking like figures from an Andrew Wyeth painting—expressive, but also soft, and vaguely impressionistic.

I always made sure the camera was at eye level with the subjects. I did this by framing the subject through the viewfinder of the camera, then stepping over to the side of the camera to make sure the camera was level and the lens exactly at the subject's eye level.

This is more important than you might think. Since there is basically nothing happening in these shots except an occasional blink and the frequent shifts of light, setting your camera and tripod should be done thoughtfully. Many tripods come with a bubble level, like on a carpenter's level, and these are worth their weight in gold. Especially with a project like this, where an angle or tilt in the camera set would distort the shot. The whole idea here was to remove everything except the subject and the light.

Direction

Directing people has never been easy for me. For one thing, I'm pretty soft-spoken and I have a hard time giving orders. I also need time to think about what I'm trying to do, and I don't want to start until I'm sure I know. This can make the people I'm working with on a project a little restless, creating some minor tension on a shoot. The Visitors helped me become more comfortable directing people—as with many lessons, through trial and error.

At first I tried tricking my subjects. I told them I was making adjustments to the camera, setting the white balance, or refocusing when I was actually rolling tape. The logic was that they'd relax and I could capture their essence more effectively than if they knew they were being filmed. Sometimes this worked, but more often it didn't. People are either compelling before the camera or they're not.

I read an interview with the artist Chuck Close, whose massive pointillist portraits have always amazed me. He described his approach to taking portraits—which he uses later in his paintings—by saying that you should never try to "capture emotion" because it's always there. In other words, emotion can't be harnessed. It's not some fleeting, elusive thing. It exists in a person, and the artist's job is to simply render it as faithfully as he or she can.

So, with that in mind, I set the shot and rolled the tape, asking only that the subject look directly into the camera. What they did in the next 15 or 20 seconds was entirely up to them.

The Edit

From a technical standpoint, there's not a whole lot that goes into editing these portraits. It's one clip butted up against the next. No fades, no dissolves. The first thing I focused on was choosing the most compelling footage from each shoot.

After logging and capturing the footage, I begin a careful review. First, I look for a good composition. I want the subject to be comfortably centered in the frame, with a sense of balance and stability. I learned about this after reading about the master painters of the Renaissance, whose portraits were composed in a triangular formation within a square frame, suggesting structural stability and balance.

I'm also looking for the most interesting moment in a shot, when the subject truly engages with the camera. I want to capture the moment when the subject's face is held balanced in light and shadow, and his or her eyes feel as if they are locking with mine.

For one series I played around with blurring the footage, as in the portrait of Brendan on page 47. I thought it gave the portraits a bit of a Rembrandt look, but I quickly came to my senses and resumed putting as little distortion as possible between the portrait and the viewer.

Finally, I made sure that each portrait had the right amount of contrast. I wanted to set my subjects' skin tones apart from the background, and this wasn't always possible with just the camera. In fact, each portrait I've shot has been color corrected. (Both Final Cut and Premiere have excellent color-correction features.)

Using Ruff's portraits as a guide I pulled the saturation down a bit, effectively pulling some of the color out of my subjects' faces. Then I increased the contrast, boosting the white value and deepening the blacks.

Look at the images on the right. Notice how much better the color-corrected version looks than the original image. It has more energy, and doesn't suffer from muddy, low contrast.

In Sum

I started The Visitors series to get better at working a new camera, but I know that there was more to it than that. I think that sometimes I have to give myself a practical reason for engaging in a project that, like this one, was personal and expressive in nature. Like so many designers I have a hard time with self-definition; am I an artist or a creative whose skills are better suited for commercial purposes? I have always been uncomfortable with the title Commercial Artist, but this project allowed me to recognize that it may be the best way to describe what I do. As a graphic designer— the "commercial" part—I have a responsibility to whatever brand I decide to do work for, but as an artist I have an equal responsibility to do what artists have always done: react and respond to the world...to send out a message. I like that the two seemingly contradictory words—"commercial" and "artist"—are joined, because they can't help but feed each other. By making time for personal work, my client work improves and becomes more creative, and my client work reminds me of the necessity of storytelling and thematic relevance in my personal work.

Recently I've been looking at the work of contemporary photographers. Philip-Lorca diCorcia, Thomas Ruff, Thomas Struth, Gregory Crewdson, Nan Goldin, and my latest favorite, Richard Avedon. I look at the light and the composition and I lose myself in the expressions and the body language of the people in the photos. Both diCorcia and Avedon have had celebrated careers as both artists and commercial magazine and fashion photographers. Looking through their work it's often hard to tell the difference between a portrait or photograph taken for commercial purposes and one taken purely for artistic purposes.

I've always been aware of just how thin the line between fine and applied art can be. Certainly a piece of graphic design like Stefan Sagmeister's *Scratch* poster all but erases that line. Long after the lecture that it was advertising took place, the work remains a lasting statement on the obsessive and painful act of creating.

For me it's crucial that I keep that line between "commercial" and "art" as thin as I can. The Visitors project reminded me to do that.

More than anything, I was reminded to keep learning from the artists I admire. They offer inspiration both in their work and in their courage to simply be artists.

Find a project you like that really emphasizes camera work, and just try to figure out how it was done. Then use that approach in a project of your own, with bits of additional inspiration thrown in, such as an earlier work of visual art, or anything else that feeds your muse.

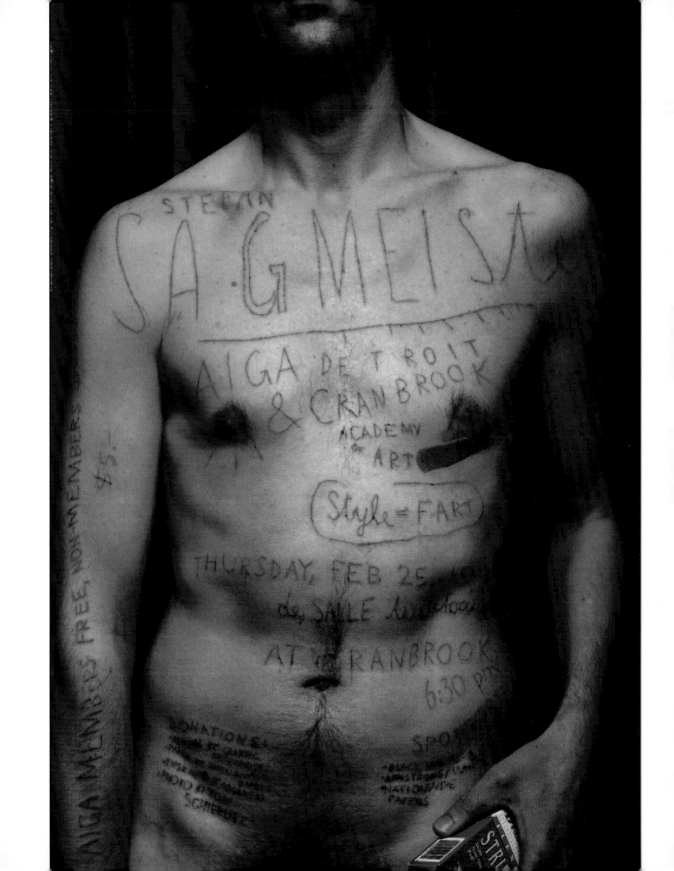

FALLING IN LOVE WITH MOVEMENT

FILMMAKING IS A CHANCE

TO LIVE MANY LIFETIMES.

—ROBERT ALTMAN

In the fall of 2004 my friend Pam Tanowitz contacted me after seeing some of the video portraits from The Visitors series. She said she was working on a project and wanted my help. Pam had recently choreographed a piece for her troupe, the Pam Tanowitz Dance Company, to perform at the Guggenheim New York in the spring of 2005. She wanted me to shoot her dancers portrait-style and screen them during the performance. The idea of combining my static video portraits with a fluid, modern dance intrigued me so I agreed straightaway.

I arranged for the dancers to come by my studio one at a time for the portrait shoot. After taking each dancer's portrait, I asked if I could film them dancing. Fortunately they all said yes. I asked them each to select their music, and they all chose something different, from the Red Hot Chili Peppers to the mellow, ethereal songs of the Cocteau Twins.

When I reviewed the footage I realized I had no identifiable thread between the dancers, aside from the simple fact that they were dancing. And even that was useless since they were all dancing to different music. I had no idea what to do with the footage. It wouldn't have made sense to edit the dancers together without some sort of unifying theme.

So I did what I often do when I'm stuck on a project: I went home, hung out with the family, and after everyone went to sleep I uncorked a bottle of red and retired to the couch, lights off, with my iPod. I skipped around to different songs, but kept coming back to a song by Mogwai—one of my favorite bands and, recently, a major artistic muse for my work. The song was "Golden Porsche," from their 2003 album *Happy Songs for Happy People*.

Like many of Mogwai's songs, "Golden Porsche" is an instrumental piece consisting of just keyboards, guitars, and drums. The song's minimalist melody builds to a sonic apex, and then dissolves. The song conveys a sense of longing, and after listening to it three or four times I started to hear a theme in it. Maybe it was the wine, maybe it was because I'd started to look through a bible my buddy Todd gave me—whatever it was, the word "rapture" popped into my head, and I couldn't shake it.

With that, I decided to use "Golden Porsche" as the score for the spot, and rapture as the theme for its nonverbal narrative.

My Obstructions

A few days before the first shoot I watched Lars von Trier's 2003 film *The Five Obstructions*, an homage to, and collaboration with, Jørgen Leth, a Danish filmmaker, sports commentator, and one of von Trier's most revered influences. Conceived by von Trier, *The Five Obstructions* revisits one of Leth's earliest works, a short from 1967 titled *The Perfect Human*, through five remakes of the original film. Von Trier instructs Leth to shoot each of the films according to strict and sometimes random guidelines—or "obstructions"—such as "no cut can be longer than twelve frames." The results are inventive and beautiful. And though the films aren't always spot-on, as a whole the project is a fascinating exercise.

Like von Trier, Leth uses self-imposed limitations to make powerful, emotive films imbued with stark realism. "When I have something to work against, it liberates my imagination," he once told the film journalist Anthony Kaufman. But as a sports commentator, he also believes that not everything can be scripted. "What I like with games is that there is this uncertain outcome and the element of chance," he said in the same interview. "When I make films, I'm very conscious about leaving space for uncertainty, and for some unexpected things. So filmmaking is also a game."

Because finding creative solutions within limitations and leaving room for uncertainty are both cornerstones of my own process, I also came up with a set of limitations.

First, I decided that I wouldn't use what I consider to be dance film clichés, such as slow motion, overlays and, especially, black and white, which just seemed too obvious. I wanted to focus only on movement and the dancers' expressions.

So, I framed up a three-quarters shot—from the waist up—so I could catch their eyes, and I directed them to freeze occasionally. This allowed me to capture a kind of portrait. As in my other video portraits, their eyes are the focal point of those shots. And those static shots contrast with the fluidity of their movements throughout the piece to create a palpable tension between the physical and the psychological.

Another goal I set for myself was to become comfortable enough with the camera to shoot in manual. This meant switching everything "auto" on the camera off: auto focus, auto zoom, auto iris and shutter speed, and auto white balance. This can be risky when you are new to using a camera: you might misfocus or forget to check your white balance as the light changes. But with manual you can dial in a much richer shot, and it forces you to stay connected with your camera throughout the shoot.

I remember when I first looked at the footage I wanted to reach through the screen and touch the dancers' skin. That might sound a little creepy, but it really isn't. Well, okay, it is a little, but I often fall in love with my subjects, and while these love affairs are one-sided and last no longer than the project itself, I wanted to communicate that feeling in the spot. So it had to be in color, specifically a warm color treatment that would emphasize the dancers' natural skin tones. I also decided to avoid transitions, such as fades to black, dissolves, and cross-fades, as well as any tricky stuff, like split screens. I wanted to build something that did nothing to compromise or in any way distract the viewer's attention from the dancers and their movements.

The Edit

Since I'd filmed each of the dancers separately, I now had to find a way to tie it all together into a single piece and create a synergy between them. I also wanted to build a narrative out of their movements. With the theme of "rapture" in mind I started looking through my footage for sections that would support that theme.

The Mogwai song follows a structure of build-up, release, and resolve. So I started cutting the spot around that structure. I started with slower, more contained movements and built from there. I also noticed that all the dancers reached towards the sky in a prayer-like gesture at various points in each of their dances. I pieced those clips together as the Mogwai song built towards its crescendo.

Dance, music, and filmmaking are all essentially about rhythm. So I never went very long without checking the piece against the song, cutting on the beat—but not exclusively. I wanted the beat to inform the spot, but I also wanted the dancers' movements to be independent of the Mogwai song. I didn't want the movement and music to be rigidly married in the spot, but rather to complement each other.

So during the editing process three things were necessary. First, to keep track of an internal rhythm based on how I felt the cuts worked with the music, but also the very technical rhythm of the song—where the kick drum was, and where the "one" on the beat was. Second, to pick out points in each reel where the dancers' movements could naturally flow from one dancer to the next. Third, to let the theme of rapture guide me during the edit. With these three guidelines, I was able to build a narrative from multiple and sometimes disparate elements.

In Sum

The Movement Study remains one of my favorite projects. I remember a line from the Steely Dan song "Deacon Blues": "I cried
when I wrote this song." This project was one of those for me. I can
get choked up watching it. That's not to say anyone else will! Still,
it felt good to create something that worked on that level for me
and the experience just furthered my commitment to filmmaking.

Jørgen Leth is quoted as saying, "For me, poetry has a strong
link to my filmmaking. My films learn from poetry. In poetry, you're
free. I have no message, I have nothing I want to tell, I just start
and I see where it leads, and it's a big surprise and a relief if it's
good. That's the ideal state for filmmaking."

In the Movement Study I didn't have a message, or anything
to tell...at first. I certainly didn't start the project with "rapture" in
mind. I just wanted to try filming something different: an extension
of my portraits. But by identifying a theme and then working to
support it, I was able to create something more. And by establishing a set of obstructions, or limitations, I think I avoided some film
clichés (nothing would have killed this spot faster than a few slow-
motion sequences in black and white). Those limitations forced
me to work harder to find the right sequences to fit together.

Jørgen Leth and Lars von Trier reminded me that filmmaking, like many other crafts, flourishes under limitations. Since the
advent of DV, limitations are fewer now than they were even ten
years ago. And while this can be wonderful, allowing for so many
more possibilities than the earliest filmmakers could have ever
fathomed, I think such boundless freedom can spoil us, too. The
best way to overcome this and rediscover the immense power
of the imagination is to impose limitations on yourself. You'll be
surprised what you can accomplish.

60 SECONDS WITH...SUM 41

I SHALL BE SO BRIEF THAT

I HAVE ALREADY FINISHED.

—SALVADOR DALI

A few years back, around 2001, I got a call from Doug Gottlieb, Creative Director at RollingStone.com. He asked me to come by his office to do a little consulting on the site's redesign. When I got there I found that Doug had nearly finished the design, and it was very good. I managed to make a few suggestions, like changing squares to circles, tightening things up a bit, and making the site more consistent; but he really didn't need much help. As we worked, bouncing ideas back and forth and trading places behind the computer, we got onto the topic of rich media online.

I was known mostly for my Flash work, so Doug asked if I'd be interested in creating some motion graphic spots in Flash to augment the musician interviews posted on RollingStone.com. I liked the concept of adding rich media to the interviews, but wasn't sure about using Flash. So I went home and thought about what I'd want to watch after reading an article about a band online. And the more I thought about it, the more the idea of using Flash seemed like the wrong thing to do.

Even back then, I was convinced that video on the Web was going to explode any minute, so I started thinking in that direction. Also, as a former musician and a huge music fan myself, I knew I'd want to see the performers caught on film and watch them in action, getting an insight into their personalities. So I called Doug and suggested that we do video. Fortunately he agreed, and we started conceiving a series of short documentaries produced exclusively for the Web.

Streaming video was in its nascent stages at the time and many of the videos showing on the Web were just repurposed content, compressed to play back online. The quality was often low and the frame sizes tiny. With this in mind, I decided that no spot could be longer than 60 seconds, not including the intro and end titles. At 60 seconds, we could present a movie with a small file size that would load and play quickly on low data rate broadband and perform acceptably on dial-up connections (which were still pretty common back then). I also felt it was an appropriate length for Web viewing. I'm a big fan of the movie trailers on the Apple.com site—and I'm clearly not the only one: the trailer page is one of the most trafficked pages on that site—and I always appreciated how the trailers could deliver a storyline, theme, and some emotional punch all in under 90 seconds. Thus the 60-second length (and title for the series). The 60-second limit also challenged us as visual storytellers to be economical—to use only the most relevant footage from a given shoot.

Two weeks later Doug called my office to ask if my staff or I had ever heard of a band called Sum 41. We hadn't, but Doug assured us they were going to be huge and asked if we'd like to shoot them for one of our 60-second video profiles. I jumped on it and hit the Web to learn about this band. Turns out Sum 41 was a very young—the members were all around 20—late '90s-style "punk" band from Ajax, Canada, a suburban community not unlike any suburb in the U.S. They were kids right out of high school, slightly clueless, sophomoric, and energetic all at the same time. And they didn't take themselves too seriously; they were full of self-deprecating humor and youthful verve.

Ultimately, these were the qualities that guided me in the final edit. But at the outset of this project, I was thinking more like a journalist and drafted a bunch of questions to ask the band. When they came by our studio a few days later, I positioned them in front of a white backdrop by a window at one end of our loft office and started to film and interview them as a group, to best capture their spontaneity and their group dynamic.

The Shoot

We set a Canon XL1 camera on sticks (tripod) directly center and about ten feet back from a white backdrop. The large loft windows flooded the area with beautiful afternoon light directly from the left. The light was somewhat diffuse due to the time of day and the fact that the windows faced east, so there was no hard, direct sunlight.

The band arrived and we spent a little time positioning them between the camera and the backdrop. My employees at the time, Ian and Matt, did most of this, with Ian directing the band members into a nice group shot.

We shot about 45 minutes of the band answering questions and expounding on them, interacting with each other, and just messing around. The natural light from my loft window wonderfully highlighted the band members' clothing, all bold-colored t-shirts—reds, blacks, and grays—which created a nice contrast to the white backdrop. Some months later, when shooting Stevie Nicks for another 60-second spot, the muted, earthy color scheme we used with her was totally appropriate. But for Sum 41 we wanted loud and bright—just like the band.

The footage itself was beautiful. And after capturing it I felt that we had good stuff to work with. But there was a problem. I had chosen the location by the loft's window solely for its light. I was thinking only of the shot, and I forgot about the other half: sound. Shooting in Manhattan, I don't just get great natural light, I also get the clamor of city streets: sirens, buses, people, car horns...you name it. And it's easy for me to get so involved with the shoot that I sometimes don't notice the noise until it's too late, when I begin the log-and-capture process.

aste my time, become another cas

A note on interviewing

It's important when interviewing a subject to avoid giving verbal feedback during his or her answer because your responses will be recorded along with your subject's voice. You have to kill your natural inclination to respond—uh-huh, yes, right, oh really, wow, etc.

Some documentary filmmakers, like Errol Morris, do this all the time to provoke their subjects, steer them in certain directions, and even to reinforce the fact that a director is present, and the film is, in fact, a documentary.

But I've found I get the best footage when I'm totally quiet, so I let plenty of time go by after asking a question. From countless cop shows, we know that detectives have used this trick for ages; they ask the suspect a question, then sit stone-faced and, without providing even a nod, allow the suspect to talk him- or herself into a corner. I don't recommend taking it this far, but you have to be able to bear some uncomfortable silences—they can often lead to revealing and spontaneous responses.

Dealing with Sound

In truth, even for a simple shoot, your best bet is to hire a professional soundman. In New York sound recordists charge anywhere from $300 to $500 a day and they bring their own gear. That may sound like a lot, but even $500 is a good idea when you think about how many hours get eaten up in the editing process trying to improve bad audio. Still, it doesn't hurt to know some sound basics, especially if you're on a tight budget.

Even with the best gear in the world and an expert sound recordist, you still won't make a noisy room quiet. When scouting for a place to shoot you should give as much attention to the ambient noise as to the way it looks. This might mean abandoning a location that otherwise would have been perfect, or it might mean turning off air conditioners, radios, telephones, cell phones and, in New York at least, radiators. Sound is half the experience of a movie—in fact a movie with shaky or imperfect images and good audio will often be seen as hip or edgy, while a movie with perfect shots and rough sound can be intolerable.

I learned this the hard way. A few months after the Sum 41 shoot I was working on another "60 Seconds with…" spot on the Canadian band Nickelback. I interviewed the band before one of their shows, backstage at the Hammerstein Ballroom in Manhattan, with one of my employees manning the camera while I shouldered the boom.

I chose a small room next to the main backstage room to shoot in, but didn't notice that the room had low ceilings lined with air vents. Air vents emit a low-frequency hum that's surprisingly loud if you stop to listen. But none of this crossed my mind at the time. I had just bought an expensive boom and shotgun mic, and I thought I had it covered. When I got back to the studio and began capturing the footage, I immediately became aware of the audio (or lack thereof). I'd captured the sound of the air vents and not much else. Nevertheless, I managed to piece the clip together, but the audio was horrible and the project was, in my mind, a failure.

With Sum 41 we used the camera's built-in microphone. The quality of built-in mics ranges from camera to camera, but unfortunately, even if the mic is great, a camera is a lousy location for a mic. This is true for a couple of reasons. First of all, a mic mounted on a camera is likely to pick up the camera's motor noises, as well as the sounds of the operator's hands shifting and working the controls. Secondly, *no* mic records very good sound when more than three feet away from the subject. So if you are relying on your camera mic to record sound, make sure you are physically as close as possible to the subject.

Also, you should never assume that your sound is good, so bring a good set of headphones and make sure someone is listening while you record.

We managed to capture useable sound with the built-in mic, mainly because the members of the band were not what you'd call soft-spoken. Still I had to pass on a few good cuts, later in the edit, because of sirens or taxi horns obscuring the voices.

The Edit

"I saw an angel in the stone and carved to set her free."
—Michelangelo

After logging and capturing the footage, I assemble a rough cut. Here I appropriate Francis Ford Coppola's scriptwriting method: when beginning a new script, Coppola says he just lets himself go—no editing, just straightforward, stream-of-consciousness prose. His intention is to purge all his ideas, good and bad, and to edit them later. I keep this in mind as I begin editing. For example, I'll start assembling an edit almost randomly, following a thread I know I'll abandon as soon as I reach an impasse, and then I'll start a new one. Or I'll assemble a number of different edits based on specific points the subject makes. I also spend time finessing a sequence I think will work as the beginning or the end, with no clear idea of the body or direction of the spot overall. The point is that I let myself free associate for a while. This helps remove the pressure of creating something great right off the bat and allows me to approach the edit intuitively.

The first roughs of my Rolling Stone films ran about four to five minutes each, gleaned from over 45 minutes of raw footage. In many ways, creating a rough is my favorite part of the process. It can be thrilling to see the story emerge. That said, it still takes a lot of patience to go back through all your footage.

It was hard enough paring 45 minutes down to a five-minute rough, but I was still a long way from 60 seconds. I recalled a great bit of wisdom from the late writer Dorothy Parker: "You have to kill all your darlings." Parker's advice echoes another of my favorite quotes, this one from Ernest Hemingway: "Write the story, take out all the good lines, and see if it still works." Both quotes remind me that what I might think is essential in a piece—things that I may even have fallen in love with during the initial editing stage—is expendable.

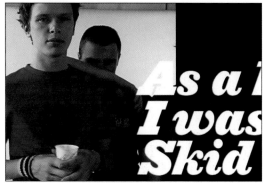

As I said above, I was struck by Sum 41's irrepressible energy right away—in their music and during the shoot. They were all over the place, moving in and out of the shot, changing positions with each other, and at one point a band member even ran to the bathroom to throw up. (It was his birthday the night before and they'd celebrated...well, like rock stars.) So I tried to mimic their energy in the edit. I deliberately chose hard cuts, where the frame composition from one cut to the next would be sudden and frenetic.

My first cut did that pretty well. But something was lacking. Having captured the band's energy, something was needed to bring the piece together.

In the final edit I remembered a poster I'd seen a few days earlier, in a window on my walk home from work, and the solution occurred to me instantly. The poster I'd seen was all angles and text—and the text itself became another angle in the design, simultaneously augmenting and reinforcing its visual aesthetic. Since one of the things that really struck me about Sum 41 was their music, specifically their entertaining lyrics, I decided to incorporate a few lines from their single "Fat Lip" into the spot. In the final edit, I superimposed lines like "casualty of society" and "I'm a no-goodnick lower middle class brat" on the band. The text became a thread that helped stitch the piece together.

This inspired me to use text in all the RollingStone.com spots. But looking back, I think Sum 41 is the best of all. The text doesn't simply tie the piece together; it becomes a strong graphic element, pushing the band around and off the screen space. This gives the spot an energy that I think underscores the energy of the band itself.

In Sum

The "60 Seconds with..." spots were like haikus, meant to convey more than I could articulate in prose—or even, perhaps, a full-length documentary. With just 60 seconds to work with, essence is all you have time for—whether of a single person, a whole band, or anything else—and that's harder than it seems.

But one minute can also be a very long time when you stop and think about it. The Lumière brothers pioneered filmmaking over a hundred years ago with one-minute films depicting scenes of everyday life, and they fascinated audiences around the world with them. With DV and the editing software available today, and enough footage to choose from, we can fascinate audiences in the same span of time. But doing this requires two equally important pieces: tuning into the essence of your subject, and then paying close attention to the details—from sound quality to every moment of footage—to best convey that essence.

Try telling a story in 30 or 90 seconds, like the best commercials or a good movie trailer. It's a wonderful exercise in restraint and helps you get into the practice of identifying those key sequences that best communicate your story.

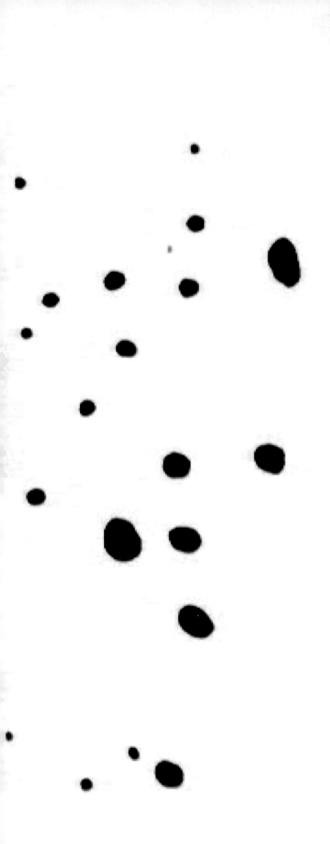

MY FAVORITE DESIGNERS

HONOR THY ERROR AS A HIDDEN INTENTION.

—BRIAN ENO AND PETER SCHMIDT

I n early 2004, Karen Tenenbaum, a Creative Director from Adobe, called me to inquire about some site design they needed. The job itself wasn't right for the studio at the time, so I declined. Karen and I had stayed close since I designed the Adobe.com site back in '99, so we took a moment to catch up and hear what each other was doing. I mentioned an idea for an online video series that would celebrate the design work of my peers. Karen was immediately interested and thought Adobe would be interested in sponsoring the series. Turns out they were, and we eventually worked out a deal. Part of the deal I made was that no designer would ever have to mention Adobe or their software; instead the spots would focus on the designer's work, process, and inspirations.

I started the series filming my friend Stefan Sagmeister, an Austrian émigré who's lived in New York the past 15 years or so. I've been a big fan of Sagmeister since I got into the business myself. More recently, we've become friends and colleagues, and in 2004 we were invited to give a couple of talks together in Texas, one at a conference in Dallas and another at the Creative Summit at Texas State University in San Marcos. We flew down, gave the Dallas talk, and headed down to San Marcos in a rented Mustang convertible. I took my camera along and shot about two hours of footage—everywhere from the airport, to the car, to Stefan's talk. Later I edited those two hours down to six or seven minutes for the final cut. My goal with Stefan was to capture his unique conceptual way of thinking, as well as his offbeat humor and quirky but approachable charm.

Next up was Paula Scher, a partner at Pentagram and another of my all-time favorite designers. Paula was a gas to hang out with and her shoot went extremely well, though I chose a location that overlooked Fifth Avenue. If you listen carefully you'll hear the roar of Midtown Manhattan throughout the spot. I went in thinking I knew a lot about Paula's work and left amazed and inspired by all that she's created in her 34 years as a designer.

Then I filmed Milton Glaser, the design legend who created the "I ♥ NY" logo and so much more over his 50-plus-year career. The spot was an honor to shoot, but difficult. I was intimidated interviewing such an iconic figure and came in with my standard questions, such as "What's your creative process?" and "Who are your influences?" Milton was polite, but seemed disinterested in such questions. I got the feeling that he'd answered these questions many times in many interviews before. We sat across from each other, me beside my tripod and Milton against a wall covered with a black backdrop. Midway through the interview I sensed we were both growing uncomfortable. So I suggested that he show me his building. I unlocked the camera from the tripod and kept the tape running as we explored the four floors of his brownstone. That's when the interview took off. We both loosened up as we looked through his countless posters, books, sketchbooks, and paintings. In the end, the hardest part was deciding what to leave in and what to take out. I'd set a time limit of seven minutes for these spots, and whenever possible I like to keep them even shorter. But with Milton there were so many inspirational moments I didn't want to let go.

Now to the one I almost botched.

Shooting James Victore

James Victore makes graphically simple yet powerful, symbolic posters, many of which are charged with controversial political themes rich with visual and thematic contrasts. Many of them consist of nothing more than a simple drawing, or even just broad strokes of black ink on a solid background—often of pure white.

In retrospect, it might have been appropriate to let a similar kind of contrast drive the shoot itself, where James, in a black t-shirt, would talk about his work in the middle of an empty white room. But that's not what I did. Instead, I went to his workspace, site unseen, to shoot him in his own environment. I hadn't scouted the location, partly because I was very busy in the days leading up to the shoot, but also because I like to allow for those fortunate accidents that lead to unexpected and beautiful results. But not all accidents are fortunate; sometimes the space you leave for serendipity results in major problems down the road.

The Death Penalty Mocks Justice

The United States remains the only Western industrialized nation to retain the death penalty and carry out executions. While the rest of the world turns its back on state-sanctioned killing, the death penalty in the U.S. continues to be applied in a racist and arbitrary manner. Capital punishment has never been implemented in a fair and non-discriminatory way. It has never been proven to be a deterrent, yet our nation's death row, and executions continue to escalate. The death penalty is a mockery of justice. In the pursuit of equality before the law it must be abolished.

The Shoot

The shoot was very simple. I used my Panasonic DVX100 camera, a tripod, and a Sennheiser ME66/K shotgun mic that I mounted on the camera. I used a short XLR cable to plug the shotgun mic into the camera's audio input.

As mentioned in the previous chapter, the problem with on-camera mics is that they are susceptible to motor and handling noise. In general it's wise to avoid using on-camera mics if possible, but it worked for me this time because I was in a quiet place and was able to get the subject—James—close to the camera.

As for lighting, I used only natural light. But I didn't take full advantage of it because I'd set up the camera in all-auto mode: auto-focus, auto-white balance, and auto-iris. I did this because at the time I still didn't feel confident enough with the camera to dial in the right settings manually. Unfortunately the resulting image suffered as the auto controls often made safe, middle-of-the-road choices...which is what they are built to do.

I had James sit at his desk and positioned the camera directly across from him, framing his sketchpad in the lower half of the shot. So far, so good. James works his ideas out by sketching, so that part of the shot made sense. But when you set up a shot, you have to think of the entire composition.

James's desk was positioned in front of a portion of his poster collection. He has one of the largest poster collections I've seen and many of them cover the walls of his workspace. The posters behind him, occupying the top half of my composition, were beautiful and I thought they'd make a fine background for the shot. But the posters were also busy, with a lot of visual information. Many were political posters, bold and designed to grab your attention, and they ended up diverting attention from the actual *subject*, James.

Another problem was the hue of my shot: James wore a brown shirt over his white t-shirt, he has brown hair, and he has an olive-toned complexion. The table was brown and his sketchbook was beige. Plus, the overriding color in the posters behind him was beige as well. The result was an almost monotone brown shot with very little contrast. This was the exact opposite of what I needed: a shot that reflected James's work, which is at once beautiful and powerful in its simplicity and use of contrast.

Depth of Field

I may have been able to create a more appealing shot of James had I tried to employ a shallow depth of field, where James appeared in sharp focus and the background—the posters—were subtly blurred. Professional cinematographers consciously control the depth of field of their shots, while amateurs tend to ignore it—if they even know what it is!

In short, depth of field refers to the range of distance from the camera that is in focus for a given shot. Depth of field is said to be deep when everything in a shot—foreground, midground, and background—is all in focus. In contrast, a shallow depth of field is one where only selected objects in the frame are in focus.

Small format video tends to offer a deep depth of field—everything is equally in focus. As a result, people sometimes refer to the video image as flat. In contrast, most Hollywood movies employ a shallow depth of field to guide the viewer's attention to specific areas of the frame—typically the protagonist, against an artfully blurred background.

This shallow depth of field can be achieved in video. As mentioned in "Getting Started," there are two and only two controls that affect DOF—on any camera. In order of importance, these are:

- The focal length of the lens—the longer/more "zoomed-in" the lens, the shallower the depth of field. In other words, to achieve a shallower DOF you can move your camera far away from your subject and zoom in on the subject.

- The iris—the more open the iris/lower the F-stop, the shallower the depth of field. Since opening the iris brightens the image, you might have to counter this by using a neutral density filter or lowering the lights.

Achieving a shallow depth of field also requires a fair amount of space—both between the camera and the subject, and between the subject and the background.

Losing a Day in Vain

I spent an entire afternoon working on a rough cut of the footage. I'd already completed the spots on Stefan Sagmeister and Paula Scher, so I figured taking the same approach with the Victore piece—focusing equally on James and his work—would be smart. At least it was familiar ground. But it wasn't working. The composition of my shot wasn't compelling.

Not only was the shot bad, I had blown the interview, too. I'd asked closed questions, and that made it difficult for James to reply with complete answers. For example, I'd said things like, "James, I really like that you put up your own rent money to print and post political posters. It seems like you're really committed to the power that design can have." I should have just said, "James, tell me about your Columbus Day poster." This could have yielded a much richer and more interesting response from the artist.

I went home frustrated, worn out, and a little depressed. I didn't think I'd be able to make anything worthwhile from what I had, and I was angry with myself for wasting so much of my and James's time. I showed the rough to my wife anyway, hoping she could shed some light on the problem—sometimes a fresh pair of eyes can work wonders. Unfortunately, she only reinforced what I already thought: the footage simply wasn't any good.

Christina said that, although she was intrigued by James's work, she couldn't see any resolution to the spot's problem. She could see how exhausted I already was at work, and suggested that I should maybe chalk this one up to experience and move on. At the very least, I knew I needed the rest of the night off. So we put our son to bed and fired up a DVD, not at all expecting what came next.

Learning from Fellini

That night we watched *La Dolce Vita*, Federico Fellini's 1960 black-and-white epic about a vacuous, celebrity-obsessed subculture in postwar Italy. Towards the end, Christina commented on the importance of the film being shot in black and white, and said it wouldn't have been nearly as good if it were in color. I asked her why, and her answer summarized the film perfectly: "The movie is about the whore and the Madonna, primitivism and modernity, rootlessness and faith," she said. "That's why everything has to be black and white. It's the *contrasts* between opposites."

Although I'd seen *La Dolce Vita* many times before, the solution to my spot on James became clear during the last scene of Fellini's film.

The final scene takes place at a beach, with everyone dressed in either black or white. The juxtaposition of beach, water, and sky accentuates the starkness of the shot even further. A shallow flume—a small tributary in which water runs out to sea—separates the leading man, who's been corrupted by the culture that surrounds him and is dressed all in white, and a comparatively virtuous woman, wearing a simple, black dress. It's a beautiful, sparse shot. And above all, it fully supports Christina's theory about contrasts.

A note on art direction

Directing is all about choices. Fellini and the film's art director, Piero Gherardi, chose to end La Dolce Vita *with two characters—a man and a woman—on a beach, standing a hundred yards apart, divided by a river. They chose to use no loud patterns or colors, just a white suit for the man and a black dress for the woman.*

I've always been aware of art direction in film-making, but until recently I never gave it enough attention in my own work. As with the Victore spot, I'd always start a given project believing I would find a suitable location for each shot. I rarely scouted locations or brought an art director.

Granted, you can't always scout a location or hire an art director. When shooting documentaries, for example, you're often filming on the run and chasing the action wherever it might go. But even documentaries can benefit enormously from basic art direction—even something as simple as placing a black backdrop behind your subject.

A Second Chance

Inspired by the final scene of *La Dolce Vita*, I wanted to call James and ask if we could do a re-shoot. I'd have sit him in the middle of his studio—dressed in all white or all black—and clear the space around the shot. Then I'd ask a number of open questions and just let it roll. But the more I thought about this, the less feasible it seemed; both of us were way too busy for another shoot.

This left me back where I started, with 30-odd minutes of problematic footage. Still, I knew I was close to a solution; I just didn't know what it was yet. The night was still relatively young. So with *La Dolce Vita* fresh in mind, I poured myself a glass of wine, put my iPod on random, and lay on the couch with the lights off. I thought about the film and my own project, and when Mogwai's song "Sine Wave" came on, my imagination hit its stride.

Like most of Mogwai's songs, "Sine Wave" starts low and mellow, and then builds to a dissonant crescendo. It consists of a warm, basic chord progression on a keyboard, coupled with a static, harsh percussion track. In fact, the song sounds just like James Victore's work *looks*: stark, dissonant, and above all, beautiful. Victore's work, like the Mogwai song, consists of just a few strokes that, taken collectively, build on one another to convey powerful, often jarring messages. Like Fellini's film, the song gave my imagination a jumpstart, setting me back on track.

I decided to lay the song down in the audio track of Final Cut Pro and re-cut the rough using "Sine Wave" as my guide. This time I would minimize the interview footage and rely more heavily on images of James's work. In short, I would create a kind of music video, comprised mainly of James's beautiful and compelling designs, interspersed with a few carefully selected clips from the interview.

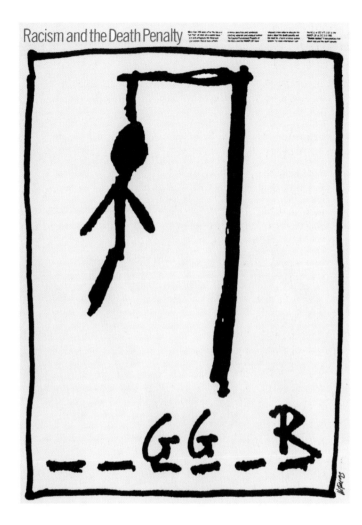

It worked. I was able to use the song's intrinsic drama to set the right mood for the spot, and also to reinforce its theme—sort of a political David and Goliath idea—with graphic design as James's sling and stone, offering an alternative to mainstream corporate and political propaganda.

The Mogwai song was also perfect because, being only three minutes long, it allowed me to re-envision the spot as a much shorter piece than the others in the series. Additionally, because the song starts very small and focused, but ends big and cacophonous, it guided my editing process as well. I married the song's rhythm to the visual rhythm in James's designs: brush strokes and paint splatters, black against white, disparate elements building to create a singular vision.

With this new approach, where I privileged the rhythms of the work and the song, I was able to use only the best sections from my interview footage. The final edit contains only four or five brief shots of James speaking. But I did lay his voice track over shots of his designs and studio space. Using just the voice track allowed me to cut a lot of the "ummms" and "ahhs" and splice together shorter and more concise responses, while at the same time to minimize my reliance on the uninteresting shot of James at his table.

Although the piece was coming together, I still had the color problem in the footage of James to deal with. No matter what I did in color correction, I couldn't increase the contrast in my muddy, brown footage. So, inspired by Fellini, I pulled the color altogether. Changing the shot to black and white allowed me to bump up the contrast. Moreover, it made thematic sense: the shot became a bit more spartan, further reflecting James's work.

A note on using tape

DV tape is cheap, and if you're involved in an intense interview, you'll kick yourself endlessly for missing gems you'll never be able to recover or recreate. One of the best parts of the interview with James was when he said, "I know my work is going to piss people off." This would have been a brilliant quote to use in the spot, but I didn't catch it because I'd let my tape run out.

Get in the habit of checking the time code, which you'll find on the viewfinder or pop-out screen, and also make a habit of switching tapes well before they have a chance to run out. I generally pull a tape anywhere from five to seven minutes before it's supposed to end. But this time I was so enthralled with the interview that I forgot and lost the moment.

Other things to keep in mind with tape:

- *Slide the "record protect" tab after you've shot to protect the tape from accidentally being recorded over.*

- *Make sure to label tapes.*

- *Make sure to keep them away from magnetic objects like speakers or the cell phone in your pocket.*

- *If a project is particularly important, consider cloning the tape—make a digital copy of it for backup. It's cheap insurance.*

Treating Still Images

For the Victore spot, like the others for this Adobe series, I wanted to highlight the artist's work. So I requested digital images from James's studio. Since the designers I'd shot up to this point were all print designers, I always got high-quality, print-ready images—usually 300 DPI (dots per inch) and in CMYK color mode, which is the mode required for the printing process. For computer screens, though, the highest resolution possible is 72 DPI and the color mode for video editing is RGB. Reconciling these two formats—incorporating digital files into a DV movie—is a multistage process.

First I open all of the images in Photoshop and convert them from CMYK to RGB and save them in a "HiRes" folder within my project folder. Then I take those RGB images and knock the resolution down to 72 DPI and save them into a folder called "LoRes." It's important to have both Hi- and LoRes versions of the images you use. As I mentioned above, I relied heavily on the actual brushstrokes in James's work, building momentum in a sequence that eventually reveals a given poster in its entirety. So I used the HiRes files for the close-ups, and saved the LoRes files for revealing the full image.

Another major issue when using digital files in DV has to do with the shape of pixels. On a computer screen, images are represented by square pixels, but with digital video, images are represented by rectangular pixels. This can cause odd sizing issues and weird proportions when you try to import images created on a computer into a digital editing program.

For example, a perfect circle created in Photoshop with a document size of 720 by 480 (the standard size of a DV image) appears as an oval when imported into your editing program. The trick is to set your document size in Photoshop to 720 by 534, instead of 720 by 480. When I knock the resolution down to 72 DPI, the size of the image changes, too, and that's when I fit the new image into the 720 by 534 document size. The example below is a poster, taller than it is wide, so I set the height to 534 and let the width be determined by that. If the image were wider than it was tall I could have set the width to 720 and let the height be automatically determined. In short, you want to size your image to either 720 or 534.

With Photoshop CS, there is an advanced option, when creating a new document, to choose between square and DV (rectangular) pixels. It also includes the ability to preview an image as it will appear on the screen with a command called Pixel Aspect Ratio Correction.

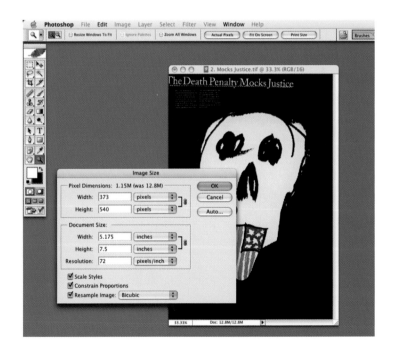

The Edit

This edit was all about working the images, sound, and live action together in a way that made sense, where each component complemented and strengthened the others. Because I was trying to minimize the live action shots and maximize the stills of James's work—all the time paying close attention to rhythm—it was crucial for me to identify the beat of the music and cut to it. I alternated between hard cuts on the beat and cuts slightly in front of or behind the beat.

In addition to making the components mesh, I also wanted to convey the visceral power of James's work, and the immediacy of his approach. No complicated processes or technological filters stand between James and his designs. His tools are simple and few: markers and pens, paper, and his own mind. He has an idea, and boom—it's on the page. To capture that immediacy, I decided to occasionally stray from the beat altogether, following my own intuition while remaining guided by the music and James's work. The result was a clear connection between the cuts and the beat, without the spot becoming predictable or rigid.

I decided not to use effects or transitions—such as dissolves, fades, or wipes—because such technical refinement would have been counter to the aesthetic of James's work. Hard cuts were simply more appropriate, and they helped me pay more attention to the film's rhythm.

In Sum

One problem with shooting documentaries is that you can get lost in the immediacy. With James Victore, I neglected to step back, give myself time, and find the right shot. It's as if I felt I had to perform the role of a quick and decisive filmmaker. I thought—as I often do—that if I'd slowed down and taken time choosing the absolute right shots, then James and his crew would get impatient, and worse, might think I didn't know what I was doing. But in my haste, I came away with footage that was just sub-par.

I'm glad I kept at it, though. What seemed like a disaster one minute became the start of a new project—one that was perhaps better than my original idea. It was a matter of letting go of my initial vision for the spot and recognizing the possibilities inherent in the footage I had.

As the saying goes, you have to lose yourself in order to find yourself—or in cases like this—lose the story to find the story.

Interestingly enough, the short I did on James Victore was actually turned down by Adobe because they felt he was too subversive and political for their corporate image—yet it got thousands of views thanks to community sites such as newstoday. com, BD4D.com, and the growing network of blogs. I mention this to stress that you don't always need corporate sponsorship to make an impact. Moreover, you should never scrap a project just because it's not what you first imagined. It can oftentimes be much more.

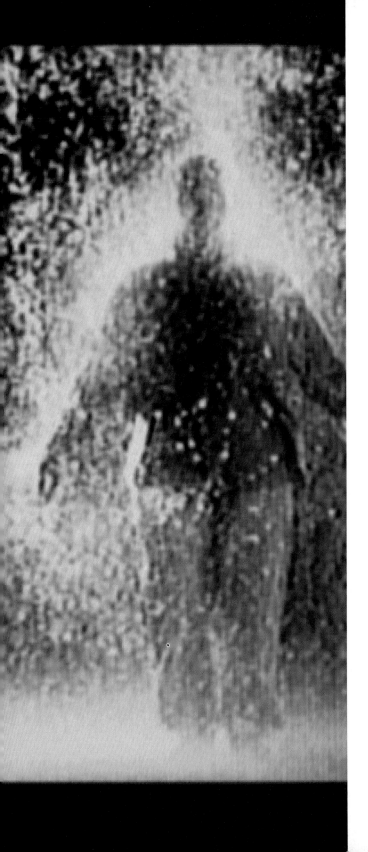

NONLINEAR STORYTELLING

GEORGES FRANJU:

BUT SURELY YOU AGREE

THAT A MOVIE SHOULD HAVE

A BEGINNING, A MIDDLE,

AND AN END.

JEAN-LUC GODARD:

CERTAINLY.

BUT NOT NECESSARILY

IN THAT ORDER.

T he idea that stories can be told outside of a "traditional" framework has always intrigued me. So, when Macromedia came out with Flash 6 in early 2002, I was excited to learn that you could treat video like any other object and write code to control it. Just as you could program text or some other object to fly across the screen, you could theoretically do the same with video.

This sparked the idea to try a nonlinear film, where the idea was that I could shoot a film, retaining control of the basic narrative through script, direction, cinematography, and editing, and then program Flash to randomly generate a playback order that is unique to each viewing. The film might start with a clip from the middle of the film, followed by a clip from the end, followed by a clip from the beginning, etc.

It would be a 21st century update of Godard's concept: not only would the narrative follow a nonlinear structure, but I, as the director, would have no control over its ultimate sequence. And while it could turn out to be a total mess, it could also be transcendent—and it would never be the same film twice.

A few years before Macromedia developed Flash 6, a handful of films were released that made a real impact on me and further inspired my interest in nonlinear filmmaking: Mike Figgis's *Time Code* (2000), David Lynch's *Mulholland Drive* (2001), and Steven Soderbergh's *The Limey* (1999). To varying degrees and to different effects, these films all follow nontraditional narrative structures.

In *Time Code*, the screen is divided into four quadrants, and each quadrant is filled with the uncut footage shot from a different camera. Each camera follows a different set of characters in the same overarching narrative. Sometimes the characters (and their corresponding cameras) share the same space, sometimes they go their separate ways. From moment to moment, the viewer is free to watch whichever character he or she wants. In a limited sense, the viewer takes over the role of editor.

The second film that inspired me was *Mulholland Drive*. Like most of Lynch's work, *Mulholland Drive* questions our perceptions of reality and dream-states, taking scenes and characters out of rational contexts and placing them in new sequences that can be both maddening and fascinating to comprehend. The story is loosely about two women who seem to swap identities, leading each of them down a dark path into subconscious desires and alternate realities, in a kind of universe parallel to their "normal" lives.

But you never know for sure if what is happening is real, a memory, or a nightmare. And you can never quite pin down the chronology of the film. Characters enter and leave without explanation, only to reappear later in very different contexts. Nowhere does Lynch provide a map for us to understand the film's disturbing and complicated plot—however much (or little) of one there is. But thematically, I think the film is consistent: It's about the disposability of the individual in the Hollywood movie machine, and how movies can so easily lure us into an unquestioning state of belief, manipulate our emotions, and play tricks on us.

Lynch constructs this theme by turning the film into a narrative dreamscape. In a dream you can start, say, submerged in water with a talking shark, and in the next instant you're walking with an ex-lover through a strange city. And not for one minute do you question the logic of it. Lynch once said, "I don't know why people expect art to make sense when they easily accept the fact that life doesn't."

Finally, Soderbergh's film, *The Limey*, portrays an aging criminal (played by Terence Stamp) recently released from decades behind bars, as he attempts to avenge his daughter's death in a seedy and decadent Los Angeles.

What I loved about the film was the non-linear way Soderbergh cut the dialogue scenes. In one scene, for example, Stamp is talking with his sidekick (Luis Guzman): Stamp is speaking one moment, and while his voice continues, the film cuts to a shot where Stamp is reacting to Guzman's response—while his original voiceover continues throughout the scene. The effect is dreamlike and disorienting, which adds very much to the atmosphere of the film and the unbalanced, temporally disconnected state of mourning in which Stamp's character resides.

MTIV Promo

The first nonlinear DV project I attempted was going to be a nonlinear Flash spot to promote my last book, *MTIV: Process, Inspiration and Practice for the New Media Designer*. My editor at the time, Steve Weiss, wanted to post the spot on the New Riders Web site. Initially I thought I'd shoot a 30-second "commercial," built in Flash and posted on the Web. Without any hard directives from Steve, I decided to experiment a little.

In an effort to come up with a concept for the ad, I started by asking myself what the book was about, but found that while I could talk about the book, I couldn't actually put those thoughts down on paper, even as a simple outline. So I decided to film myself simply answering the question, "What's the book about?"

One night, I set up my camera on our dining room table. I had Christina operate it so I could focus more on my part—playing the interviewee. She did a great job of coaxing focused answers from me and keeping me on track as I rambled on about the book.

Later I edited the footage and, in Flash, scripted up a simple random player (see the appendix) that lets the user choose between a linear (my edit) and a nonlinear (random edit) cut. If the user chooses nonlinear, the film plays in a different order every time. The theme remains the same, as does the story in this case, but each viewing registers a very different emotional impact. In a way, each viewing of the film becomes a unique experience for the viewer. But getting to this point wasn't easy.

The Shoot

The shoot was haphazard and spontaneous. I placed the camera (at that time a Canon XL1—another very good three-chip camera) on a tripod and positioned it on our dining room table. I then framed up a three-quarter shot (from the waist up) of me standing in front of a giant original poster for Michelangelo Antonioni's 1966 film *Blow-Up*. Then, noticing that the light was bad—our dining room was lit with a single 60-watt bulb—I brought in a table lamp and set it on the floor to my right. We used the on-camera mics with everything on "auto," and rolled the tape.

Christina wasn't used to operating the camera and often made sudden pans and zooms in attempts to diversify the shot. But rather than creating a problem I'd have to fix in the edit, this worked to my advantage; in limited doses, those effects looked like planned stylistic choices. They gave the shot more energy than if the footage had been more controlled.

The Edit

I started the edit aiming for the 30-second commercial I'd first imagined, but neither the footage nor the "talent" (me) was compelling enough to pare down to such a tight piece. Plus I couldn't get a cohesive story together. I was rambling in all of the footage, trying to express my thoughts at the moment, and there's a lot of uncertainty in my delivery. It just didn't translate into a straight 30-second cut.

So I decided to highlight this uncertainty. I also started to pay more attention to, and finally include, footage taken right before and after a "take"—short sections in which I'm talking to Christina about what I just said, what I should try to say, or how I should say it. In the final piece you can hear Christina's voice, off-screen, instructing me to not ramble, to "just stop when you feel yourself going too long."

When I combined those candid moments of instruction with a few of the quick pans and zooms Christina had made when framing a new shot, I realized I could create a more personal feel for the spot. One that made the actual process of creating the short visible—which essentially was what the book was all about.

And while this made the spot more intimate and engaging, it still felt a bit monotonous to watch me in front of a poster for 30 seconds straight. In an effort to break up this monotony, and to promote the book in a more immediate way, I incorporated images from the book into the piece. By cutting back and forth between me speaking about the book, and the book itself—with beautiful images of the work of artists such as Paula Scher and Bill Viola—the spot became much more substantive and visually interesting.

I went into both the shoot and the edit aiming for one thing, and by including Christina's direction and camera work, as well as images from the book itself, and by working with and not fighting my general discomfort in front of the camera, I was able to turn the spot into something much better than the promo I'd first envisioned.

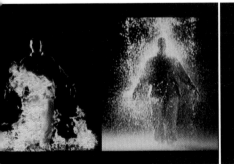

nobody not even the rain

has such small hands

Disrupting the Flow

After I completed my edit, I exported a streamline of it. Then I exported it again, but this time I exported every clip—each sequence of footage—as a single streamline until I had a folder with nine separate QuickTime movies. I then converted each of these clips into .swf (Flash player) files and placed them, along with a simple Flash "parent" movie—which acts as a holder for the individual clips—into a new folder. This parent movie also contains the code that generates a random play order for the nine different clips. In other words, it's coded to first generate a playback order, and then load the clips in that order and play them. It's a lot like the "shuffle" feature on an iPod.

The results are twofold: a linear and a nonlinear edit. Both versions work well, but I'm most excited about the nonlinear edit. It does have one performance issue that I'm not happy about—the entire film has to load before a random playback can be generated. But for a short piece like this, it's not a real problem. Once the film loads, it really holds the viewer's interest; I was surprised at how many times I watched the film, pushing the Play Random button again and again to view a new version of it. This repeated watching is, in a very practical way, the whole point of making this promo spot: to get viewings of the film. And I often need that practical reason in order to justify embarking on a new project. In truth, though, I was simply curious to experiment with this type of storytelling and to see how a random story generator works.

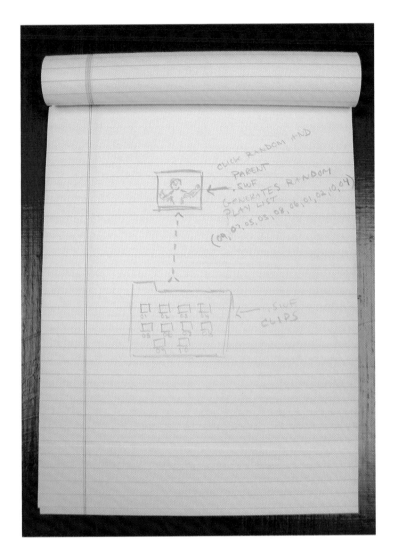

Girls Against Boys

If there is one magazine that really got me excited about digital filmmaking when I was just starting out in DV, it was *RES*. A New Media art and film magazine, *RES* was founded in San Francisco during the mid-1990s. The magazine's focus has been squarely on DV from the start, and its tone was (and continues to be) so confident and excited about the prospect of digital filmmaking in those fledgling years. You couldn't read an issue without wanting to go out a buy a camera—or at least I couldn't.

In one of its early issues the magazine featured an interview with Mike Figgis, whose film *Leaving Las Vegas* made him famous among independent and mainstream film buffs alike. The interview focused heavily on *Time Code*. As I read, I became excited by his innovative multi-channeled approach to narrative where, theoretically, it's possible to watch the movie in countless combinations, leading to just as many interpretations.

I had just finished my first music video for Girls Against Boys, and one of my clients at the time, RollingStone.com, suggested I do a short video interview on the band to accompany an online article they were producing on them. I accepted and, still buzzed by *Time Code*, began formulating concepts.

From shooting the music video, I had gotten to know quite a bit about the band. Their story wasn't much different from that of most bands. They started out as teenagers playing Who covers in each others' basements, and worked their way up: first to a release through a small indie label, then to various tours in old beat-up vans, and finally to a major record deal.

What was interesting, however, was the relationship the four guys had with each other. They'd often interrupt one another, finish each other's sentences, and just keep going. This amazed me. I was in a few bands in my twenties, and they were all dysfunctional. They all ended badly, with hot arguments and deep-seated resentments that I still regret. But these guys were different. They'd grown up together and had been playing music together for twenty years; they were a family with a shared history.

Moreover, they communicated like a band plays music: finishing someone else's phrase, adding to it, riffing off each other. You could tell they really respected one another. And they knew each other so well that they could all talk out of turn and basically wind up saying the same thing. So I decided that this intimacy and shared history was what the spot should be about.

I started thinking about *Time Code* and how I might capture the same effect, so I decided to use a split-screen technique. This allowed me to condense the film down to just over a minute while still allowing enough screen time for each of the four individual personalities. Most importantly, the split screen proved the best way to tell the story I wanted to tell, that of four guys who know each other so well that the band's interpersonal dynamic creates its own kind of energy—like a song that comes out of nowhere during an impromptu jam session.

The Shoot

We set up almost the exact same shot we'd used for the "60 Seconds with...Sum 41" shoot: camera, tripod, and white backdrop. The only major difference was that we did this shot at night, so we used two Tota lights with umbrellas. Also, for the Sum 41 shot I had intentionally placed the set next to the windows to take advantage of the natural light, failing to notice the street noise that would later compromise the spot's sound quality. To make sure we got better audio this time around, we moved the set to the back of the studio, away from the window. We set the Tota lights about ten feet away on either side of the camera and angled them directly at the center of the backdrop.

Then we conducted each interview—one band member at a time—but asked exactly the same questions in the same order, since the concept was to have them tell their story collectively. We also taped an X on the floor so each member would appear in the same spot. In the edit later, this worked perfectly: when I cut quickly between band members, there was minimal distraction.

Because we did the shoot at night—thus needing artificial lighting—our challenge was to light without casting hard shadows on the white backdrop. To best do this, we set my camera on a tripod and centered it directly in front of a given subject. We used a full shot (full body) and left enough room between the subjects and the background such that we could adjust the lights so they wouldn't create shadows.

In retrospect the shot would have been easier had I used a couple more lights to light the background and the subject separately.

A note on shadows and compression

A shadow on a backdrop would use up a considerable amount of the compressor's energy. Remember, a compression program isn't able to determine the focal point of your shot—it just sees pixels and tries to identify blocks of them that are close enough in color to be compressed into one color, thus lessening the amount of information that has to be squeezed through an Internet line.

Think of it this way: each frame you shoot has to be compressed for Web streaming and playback, and the compressor sets a limit for the amount of information each frame can hold in order to maintain a reasonable file size. So the less visual information in your shot, the less compression is required, which translates to a cleaner post-compression spot.

The Edit

After I had captured all my footage, I organized the clips based on which question was being answered. I made four different rough cuts from those clips—one for each band member as he told their story. Then I looked for places in those rough cuts where the band members were talking about the same things. I was searching for clips that I could pair up on the split screen and clips that I could string together to effectively create a sentence started by one member, picked up by the next, and so on. After that it became a matter of laying out the clips, cropping them to fit side-by-side on the screen, and experimenting until I found the right connections from one clip to the next.

Though the band's story provided a strong map for the edit—with its beginning, middle, and end—the most important things I kept in mind during this process were the themes I'd already identified: "family" and "shared history." I wanted the spot to be about how, through intimacy and familiarity, people can grow to resemble each other over time. I conveyed those themes by pairing up clips in which the members' body language, words, or facial expressions reveal that level of familiarity.

When I had a decent cut, I turned my attention to the audio. There are many sections in the film where two members are sharing the screen and speaking at the same time. In these cases I would subtly raise the volume of one voice and lower that of the other, slightly drawing attention to a phrase or word that best communicated the band's story.

But I kept it at a minimum. I wanted to make something that would be different each time it was viewed, depending on which band members the viewer chose to focus on. If I boosted one band member's volume too much I would lose that, and create instead a very linear, controlled experience for the viewer—exactly what I didn't want.

In Sum

One of the reasons I am so focused on the Web is that it often seems like a public sketchbook, where you can take an idea and quickly realize it for everyone to see. And if the idea is good it will be adopted by thousands, each adding their own talents and ideas to it. I have witnessed this in the Web design community many times.

The code-driven random playback of the *MTIV* promo just scratches the surface of what is possible for nonlinear storytelling online. Another possibility could be to shoot the individual scenes of a larger story and allow the user to choose which one to view and in what order, allowing the story not so much to change, but to become a puzzle of sorts.

With the Girls Against Boys spot I was able to employ the split screen as a thematic element. The band's story, which wasn't really that unique or interesting, became secondary to the way the individuals were shown telling it in a seamless chronology. What was interesting in the band's rendering of this story was that it showed how a rock band, much like a family, will develop its own mythology. Over time, mostly through the process of talking to the press, each band member will buy in to this mythology. This story of the band's beginnings serves as a way for the group to form a cohesive whole, through the telling and retelling of a tale that each band member knows by heart. I know from my own history in rock bands how this process helps to solidify the bond between band members. I thought the split screen really showed this phenomenon: how a band can become almost one person, its own organic entity, which we see again and again on shows like VH1's "Behind the Music" or documentaries like *Metallica: Some Kind of Monster*.

STRIKING OUT AS A MUSIC
VIDEO DIRECTOR

STRAIN AND HUMILIATION ARE

Hillman Curtis

ESSENTIAL PARTS OF FILMMAKING.

—WERNER HERZOG

Right around 2002, I started thinking about making music videos. It seemed kind of glamorous, but that was only part of the attraction. I knew I wanted to move into more film work, so I thought shooting videos would be good experience; so many of the directors I admire started out doing videos for rock bands—Michel Gondry, Spike Jonze, Jonathan Glaser—and I wanted to see if there were valuable lessons to be learned from the form. Also, being an ex-musician, I figured it would be a breeze.

For the experience and exposure, I decided to look for some pro bono music video work. I started cold-calling some of the New York independent labels like Matador and Definitive Jux, but that didn't lead anywhere. I had a friend, Eli Janney, who is the keyboardist for the New York indie band Girls Against Boys. Eli introduced me to the band after a rehearsal. We walked to a bar in Williamsburg, Brooklyn, and had a beer. I told them a bit about my background and basically asked if they would let me shoot a music video for them. They agreed and their song "Basstation" became my first project.

Though originally from Washington D.C., Girls Against Boys is a quintessential New York band: they're hard, gritty, and sexy. The four guys in the band have known each other for a long time—some twenty years—and they've developed a seamless sound that really captures the energy of lower Manhattan. I saw them perform a couple of times and was blown away by their live show. If I could reflect that energy in the video, I thought, it would be perfect. Beyond that, I didn't think of any narrative, concept, or theme.

I was right to want to mirror the energy of "Basstation," but the video could have been much richer and more interesting had I conceived a deeper idea from the start. Maybe not a full narrative, with a beginning, middle, and end; but there could have at least been a strong concept.

In retrospect I realize that I was following the lead of video director cum filmmaker Mark Romanek, whose music video work is phenomenal. His music videos don't really have stories in the traditional sense—just settings that communicate strong themes. In his video for Johnny Cash's "Hurt," for example, Cash sings in a dark museum-like room, with his wife, June, nearby. The setting is beautiful, and it reflects the melancholy tone of the song and the severity of Cash himself.

In that same spirit—wanting the energy to reflect the song's spirit—I rented a loft for one day in a grimy part of Chinatown, and did the whole shoot in an afternoon. The space couldn't have been better: it was raw—just like the band's sound—and it had this great old rickety elevator, which I just had to use. Everything about the space said "downtown."

The Shoot

"You can't go off half cocked and shoot and shoot and shoot,
and hope that sometime after you finish shooting you can
cobble together all the pieces and get a film out of it."
—Jake Eberts, Producer, *Dances with Wolves*, *Gandhi*,
Driving Miss Daisy, *Chariots of Fire*, and more

All in all, I did the shoot for under $1,000, including pizza—spending
the majority on the $800 loft rental. In keeping with the stripped-
down aesthetic of both the band and the loft space, I shot the
video with just two cameras—a Canon XL1 we outfitted with a
wide-angle lens, and a cheap, one-chip consumer camera. My
associate, Ian Kovalik, put the one-chip camera on a tripod right in
front of the band for the master shot and we took turns during the
shoot walking around the loft with the better Canon XL1.

We happily figured that we could just show up at the loft with
a box of DV tapes, hit the "record" buttons on our cameras, and
yell "Action!" So, we plugged a CD player into a PA system and,
blasting the song, had the band play along with it seven or eight
times to make sure we'd have enough footage to work with in the
edit. Miraculously, this worked—but only because we were dealing
with a band loaded with charisma.

Even so, we could have streamlined the process considerably,
saving a lot of time in the final edit, if we'd made just a few direc-
torial decisions in advance. Just the simplest things would have
made a huge difference: decorating the loft a bit, or establishing
beforehand a few shots we knew we'd need.

A note about DV versus film

It's both a blessing and a curse that you can shoot DV on such a low budget.

On the one hand, you don't have to pay an arm and a leg for a reel of 16mm film. My cousin, Sid Hillman, shooting a video for his band, could only afford 15 minutes of 16mm film stock, so he had to be extremely well prepared to shoot only what was necessary. This meant a great deal of pre-planning and storyboarding. When I shot Girls Against Boys, I could afford to be spontaneous simply because I had so much more stock.

On the other hand, with virtually unlimited tape, you can easily over-shoot your subject, as I found with Girls Against Boys. This means a lot more work later on in the log-and-capture process, when you have to comb through all your footage to find salvageable parts.

The Edit

When I cut the spot with another associate, Adam Fox, whose experience as an editor exceeds my own, I realized that I had a lot of good material, but nothing that would hold a viewer's attention for the whole song.

So I turned the bulk of the edit over to Adam, letting him assemble a rough cut, while I started toying around with effects and colorization on select sequences. I am generally hesitant to use effects or too many filters; I prefer a straight, simple cut that tells a story without any distracting or gratuitous effects. However, the effects and color I eventually dialed in fit with a thematic direction I decided to pursue after watching an old favorite movie again.

The movie was Adrian Lyne's 1990 film *Jacob's Ladder*—a story about a Vietnam vet, Jacob (Tim Robbins), who, several years after the war, finds himself haunted by demons everywhere he goes. Lyne set the film in Brooklyn during the late 1970s, capitalizing on the harsh locations of dingy subways and old, run-down tenement apartments. To represent the demons that haunt Jake, Lyne spliced together ultra-fast cuts of people's heads moving back-and-forth, and up-and-down, to create a jarring, inhuman effect.

I was thinking about how well Lyne captured the toughness of New York, not just through the locations he chose, but also through the visual effects he used sparingly and always in the right places. I wanted to capture a similar effect in my piece, so I decided to use the same visual flourish that Lyne used to represent the demons in order to provide a visual for the band's rhythm and energy. I did this by isolating a few frames of a band member—perhaps leaning from one side to the other—and cutting back and forth trying to sync the cuts to the beat.

Adam's talents came in handy here, putting together a good rough cut and then adding some effective creative touches, like a slight vignette effect, which gave the film an old photo look where the edges of the frame have darkened over time. We also desaturated the footage, rendering it almost black and white, keeping just enough color to give it a distinctive, gritty look.

Getting a good look was one thing, but putting the edit together—as a whole—was another. Since we shot the band with absolutely no plan in place we ended up with footage that made no distinction between the song's verses, choruses, and bridge. It all basically looked the same. So we tried to establish some semblance of consistency by attempting to make the verses more staid with less cuts and longer shots and the choruses more frenetic with faster cuts. Even this wasn't totally successful because our footage, though exhaustive, was often poorly shot. In fact, I had to use an extreme letterbox, or widescreen, filter to mask ceiling fans and other things that I thought detracted from the image.

The video proved to be a success, outperforming videos produced by major studios for 100 times the cost, many of which never make it out of record company basements. It played on MTV2, Refuse TV, MuchMusic Canada, and MTV all over Europe. Equally important were the online viewings, which numbered around 20,000. The point is that for indie bands that travel in a van and load their own gear, a low budget DV video with good online traffic is a godsend, as it has the power to expose them to countless new fans.

Following the Buzz, Not My Heart

About four months after the Girls Against Boys video, and buoyed by its surprising success, I thought I'd try another one—and this time I'd try coming up with a concept before hitting the "record" button on the camera. I'd heard that one of my favorite bands of the late 1990s, Creeper Lagoon, was coming out with a new album, and I pitched the band's record company, Arena Rock Records in Brooklyn, the idea of a music video for one of their songs. It turned out that it wasn't a new Creeper Lagoon album, but a side project by one member of the band. Arena then pitched a different idea back to me. They said their main act, a southern band called Superdrag, wanted a video for their single "The Staggering Genius," and they asked me to shoot it. Although I'd never been into the band, I was seduced by those two words: *main act*. I accepted the job, figuring that if it turned out well, more "major" opportunities would be sure to follow.

I made two mistakes early on. First, I was volunteering my time, and my rule when doing that is that I should be truly passionate about the project. I had no history with Superdrag and knew none of their songs. I listened to their latest album, *Last Call for Vitriol*, and though the band is clearly talented, they just weren't my style. But they had a decent amount of buzz and I thought the project could be a stepping stone.

A note on heart

This is important: The real mistake I made in this case was not necessarily that I took the job; it was that I went into it with the wrong attitude. I once gave a talk called "Putting Your Heart into Design" at a design school in Connecticut, and one of the students asked me what advice I had for people who, just starting out, will no doubt be doing the same things all the time, just churning out banner ads—or like me, when I started at Macromedia years ago, building executive presentations over and over. "How do you put your heart into that?" he asked.

I told him about my first year at Macromedia, about the corporate presentations that consisted mainly of bullet points, pie graphs, and dull charts. I told him that I decided to focus on the exactitude of each design, and made each pixel as perfect as I could. I got deep into exploring the Swiss designer Josef Müller-Brockmann and grids. I focused on typography and consistency in design. And through all of the repetition I became aware of the power of restraint and simplicity. On the few occasions that I incorporated motion, I was always very conservative and moved elements in ways that reflected the theme of the presentation. They were not simply gratuitous.

I came to believe that even though a viewer might not be able to point to the screen and indicate exactly where an element had moved two pixels from page to page in a presentation or Web site, he or she could sense it, and too many of those mistakes could leave the viewer with a feeling of imbalance. I explained all of this to the student. When I was finished he replied, "So, rather than just taking on jobs you can put your heart into, you should find a way to put your heart into everything you do." Which was a wonderful way to put it.

My second mistake was not following my own philosophy regarding proper research and familiarity with the subject. In both my documentaries and corporate work, I always research my subjects or brands before starting a project to better understand their values and who they are, identify a story, or determine a theme. But on this project, I didn't take the time to research the band at all; instead I quickly fashioned a concept solely around their song's upbeat, chunky chords and poppy sound. In an attempt to capture the song's energy, I envisioned people just sort of dancing around in a clean white room, reacting to the song's big power chords. It wasn't that far off from those Gap ads, where people and performers moved and danced in a seamless white room, or even the Apple "switch" ads. I remember feeling really confident about my concept, which can only mean someone was dosing my coffee with Prozac.

Once I hit on the concept, I sort of ignored the song's lyrics: it is a serious song about an alcoholic. Obviously, I had missed the song's real message.

I presented the concept to the band and they accepted it. They might have been a little skeptical, but they assumed I knew what I was doing.

The Shoot

I rented a cyc room—a room that's all white and has no seams or corners—for $1,500. I wanted the band to look like the Buzzcocks on their first record cover: just four guys in a stark, white room. We brought two Canon XL1 cameras and, like the Girls Against Boys shoot, set one on a tripod and handheld the other. My plan was to shoot the band first, with the dancers I'd hired coming later in the day.

It was early in the morning when the band pulled up in their van and unloaded their gear. The guys in the band were exceptionally gracious, but shooting them was only good, not great. We had them perform/lip-sync the song four or five times. They performed well, but there were no theatrics. Where Girls Against Boys were all sinewy confidence and charisma— with Eli the keyboardist jumping around like a psychotic monkey—these guys had their feet planted in the same spot from start to finish. Actually, the band's singer, John, got into it, but the other guys were fairly placid throughout the shoot. Maybe they were unaccustomed to performing so early in the morning, and I didn't take the initiative to inspire them.

A note on directing

Directing is much more than a technical job concerned with camera angles and lighting. It is the director's job to inspire everyone on the set—both crew and talent—to deliver.

As I mentioned in "The Visitors," this isn't always easy for me. I'm fairly soft-spoken and I dislike the idea of barking orders in an effort to maintain complete and authoritative control over the set and the film. I like to work more intuitively and in collaboration with those involved. In my design work, I always include the client in the creative process. As long as the concept and goal of the project are established and agreed upon at the outset, that collaboration can be immensely helpful. Ideas are tossed around, and the original vision is often transformed into a much richer and more interesting piece.

In my filmmaking, I have a similar approach. With both the crew and the talent, as long as there is a common understanding and respect for the direction of the piece—an important component of the collaborative process—I'm eager to listen and incorporate their ideas into the film. And it's in this collaboration—where we all respect each other and the film—that the inspiration comes...for everyone involved. Everyone has a voice, everyone is heard, and everyone is moving towards the same goal. If you've done your job as a director, then you, the crew, and the talent should all feel like, as Sidney Lumet writes in Making Movies, *"we're all making the same movie."*

Then we brought in the dancers. These were actually "non-equity" actors—or actors who haven't earned their union cards, and therefore can perform without pay. We found them by placing an ad in *Backstage*, a New York trade paper—and got *a lot* of responses. We eventually chose 20 out of the 100 or so applicants.

We explained to the actors what we were after, which wasn't much—just a loose and energetic interpretation of the song's energy. The actors dove into the exercise without hesitation and, unlike the band, had no inhibitions whatsoever. But because the song sounds so lighthearted and upbeat the first time you listen to it, the dancers misinterpreted it just as I had. They flailed, jumped, rolled on the ground, and broke into erratic movements. Even the band was yelling for more. All in all, we were having a great time; it was only later while capturing the footage that I started to realize the weakness of my concept.

One of the major problems with trying to capture and sustain the energy of the song was that it was over four minutes long; stretching shots of the band and dancers over that amount of time simply wasn't interesting. It became repetitive and boring. If the song had been two and a half minutes, I might have gotten away with it. But four plus? No way.

I've seen videos where this has worked. For example, Hype Williams's video for Q-Tip's "Vivrant Thing" consists of just the rapper performing the song while a very attractive woman dances along. And it's great. Williams is a great video director: his camera work is superb, and his art direction and set design are off the hook. Also, Q-Tip is a very charismatic performer—and a proven actor to boot. Add an equally charismatic dancer/actress to the mix, not to mention a jumping song, and the video is amazing.

But I was new to music video directing, had given very little thought to set design and art direction, and was working with a power pop song about an alcoholic (which I hadn't acknowledged fully at the time). What did my unpaid dancing actors have to do with a raging alcoholic? Nothing. Dancing *bears* and alcoholics, maybe, but I had clearly struck out with this "concept"—and the resulting shoot.

The Edit

The edit wasn't any better, and it didn't save the video. In retrospect I should have followed my gut and thrown in the towel, called the band and told them I'd blown it. It's awful to review the same footage over and over, knowing full well you're not going to see anything new, and realizing that the footage itself simply isn't any good.

I decided to take a break from the video and turn my focus to client work I'd fallen behind on. I handed the edit over to Adam Fox, who had helped out so much on the Girls Against Boys video, and hoped he could straighten it out. He got a lot closer than I did, and for a second I started to believe we'd actually pull this one off. But as we finessed the edit we agreed that the piece was simply flat, that it just wasn't going anywhere. The band wasn't interesting on camera, and though each dancer had his or her own moments, they failed to add up to make the piece compelling. And the worst part for me was that my utter lack of a concept was completely obvious.

So we did what many desperate filmmakers do in this situation: we turned to effects and filters. I slathered on a strobe light and Adam went to town with a flash-bulb effect. Then I threw in some gratuitous graphics and text just for safe measure. Finally we colorized the spot, which actually looked great—except that it was totally wrong for the band. We made the image super-contrasted and blown out, making the saturation of skin tones almost nonexistent. This made for a dramatic but cold look. It didn't reflect the band's southern roots or their indie power pop sound. The colorization, just like the dancers, the weak concept, and the other effects, was simply wrong.

And here's where I made maybe my biggest mistake. I began to convince myself that the spot was good. I started to actually fall prey to the flash and the strobe and the goofy and sometimes sexy dancers. I fell in love with my colorization of the spot. (In case you've never been to therapy, this is called Denial.) Worse yet is that I began to shift the blame of my own incompetence onto the band. (Projection.) Since I basically funded the project, produced it, hired the dancers, and put so many unhappy hours into the edit, I started to believe the band should be grateful for this shiny new video. (Delusion.) Admittedly, the spot did look very professional and there were moments when it took flight, but deep in my heart I knew it was a failure; in that moment of realization I made the irrational decision to deny that. (Again, Denial, with a hint of Narcissism.)

When I showed the final cut to the band, they were pretty unhappy; to them the song was serious and personal, and I'd made it into this goofy dance thing. At that point I should have listened to their criticisms and been honest about my problems with the piece. Instead, I defended the video and things got heated. The project stalled. The record company and the band had no interest in doing anything with the video, and I stubbornly refused to change it. Looking back, a simple cut of the band alone—sans effects, hyper-color, and dancers—would have served everyone better. I'm sure that I could re-cut the spot today and find all sorts of possibilities within the limitations of my initial footage. In fact, I'd probably produce a decent spot. It wouldn't be a home run—maybe not even a double—but it certainly wouldn't be the strikeout I made the first time around.

In Sum

Finding a point-of-entry with any subject: you have to determine some aspect that you can relate to, or that you can build a story around. Girls Against Boys represented gritty New York, just like *Jacob's Ladder*, so that drove the design process. With Superdrag, I should have listened to what they were trying to say, both as a band and in the song, and then used those impressions to build a concept. Instead I did what I despise, which was to try and fool the viewer with sparkles and glitter. It was disrespectful not only to myself but to the band and their song.

Follow your heart when considering "next step" projects—those projects you pursue to make a change or stretch your abilities to that next level. It takes faith and courage to say, "This is what I am going to do," and then actually do it. For me, making those sorts of proclamations and sticking to them is difficult for a couple of reasons: I am afraid of falling on my face and I can easily get sidetracked by other opportunities—like a corporate design job that comes with a juicy budget. Knowing this—that it's already easy enough to avoid or abandon "next step" projects—I should have passed on the Superdrag video and waited for an opportunity that would have been better for me. That said, once I agreed to do the video I should have found a way to put my heart in the project. The best way to do that, I have found, is to involve yourself in your client's story. Try to understand them and seek out those universal themes that exist in every story. Superdrag is an indie band from the south, and their lead singer and songwriter, John Davis, struggled for years with alcoholism. I learned this well after I struck out on the video, but it was information available from the start that could have informed a more appropriate concept and perhaps a more personal approach.

MAKING A MOVIE

I DON'T BELIEVE IN TOTAL

FREEDOM FOR THE ARTIST.

LEFT ON HIS OWN, FREE TO DO

ANYTHING HE LIKES, THE ARTIST

ENDS UP DOING NOTHING AT ALL.

IF THERE'S ONE THING THAT'S DANGEROUS FOR AN ARTIST, IT'S PRECISELY THIS QUESTION OF TOTAL FREEDOM, WAITING FOR INSPIRATION AND THE REST OF IT.

—FEDERICO FELLINI

I have always wanted to make movies. When I was in university in the midwest—before I dropped out—I studied film theory. I remember writing papers on the films we'd seen and having them all come back marked with A's. It was easy for me and I remember thinking, "This is what I should do." At the time I wasn't sure what "it" was; I just felt that I belonged in movie-making. At 20 years old, the world seemed spread out before me, and when those papers came back with the professors' "Keep up the good work!" next to the A, I read it as a sign. But soon a stronger sign—in the form of the Ramones playing live in a small Iowa gymnasium with me pressed up against the stage—appeared before me and indicated that perhaps I should become a punk rock musician in New York or San Francisco instead (I chose San Francisco). The musician sign seemed way sexier, and came with a bus ticket out of Iowa, so I followed it. I ended up following it throughout my twenties. Shortly after my twenties ended, so did my music career. I was dropped by my label and so began my career as a graphic designer. Now some twenty-odd years later I have finally made a movie, complete with a script and actors. Granted, it's short—really just a seven-minute one-act story—and it won't set the Academy on fire, but I'm happy with it and it was a blast to make.

My justification for making this movie—the practical reason I gave myself to do it—was that it was specifically for this book. Looking over my finished chapters, I realized I'd covered documentaries, video art, and music videos, but no narrative. Writing a script and shooting actors was something I'd wanted to do for a while and had simply never made the time for. Many of my filmmaker heroes—Woody Allen, Fellini, Soderbergh, P.T. Anderson, Wes Anderson—were all *auteurs*, meaning they wrote as well as directed their films. That's what I was most attracted to, but as each year went by and I got older it became harder to try such a project. What was discouraging was that most of those filmmakers were much younger than I when they made their first films. And I was equally daunted by the complexity of the project itself: I'd need a script, decent actors, and locations, and then I'd need to figure out how to shoot it.

In order to complete the project, I knew I'd have to keep it as simple as possible. It would have to be fairly short, with only a handful of actors and very few locations. I also kept my expectations low, identifying myself as a first timer and proceeding accordingly. And by giving myself a practical reason to make this film, I was able to dive in with the knowledge that regardless of whether the short turned out well or not, the important thing was going through the process and learning, and then passing these lessons on.

I also got help from Ben Wolf, whom I'd met years ago when I took a class that he taught on cinematography. He generously led me through the process of creating my first narrative film: first we talked over coffee, then he signed on as the cinematographer and assistant director for the film. Finally, it helped to live in New York, where I could quickly find highly talented and experienced actors.

The Script

I started writing the script myself after soliciting all of my writer friends for one. I laid out parameters to the writers—one location, two people, less than 8 minutes—and never heard from most of them again. I got a few contenders, but nothing knocked me out. One of them, though, from David Alm, who is helping with this book, presented a reasonable premise: a man and a woman, ex-lovers, come together again for one evening. At the time, my wife and I were engaged in a debate about whether to stay in New York or move back west where we're from. This had been going on for months and we had become quite polarized, with me lobbying for New York and Christina pushing for Portland. There developed this impassable divide between us, and the debate infiltrated everything we did. I found myself making references to how dull the west coast was, making little jokes at any given opportunity. So when I started writing around this premise of ex-lovers meeting for a night, our debate—left coast vs. east coast—pushed its way into the work.

In my script, the woman flies from California to New York for a long weekend and visits, for a night, her ex, who moved there. They enter his dining room, having just come from watching Fellini's *La Dolce Vita*. Most of the film takes place at the dining room table, with him on one side and her on the other. They start talking and begin to tell their story metaphorically through the film. In the last scene of *La Dolce Vita*, Marcello Mastroianni is on a beach with his "friends," a degenerate and loveless group, when he sees a young virginal woman calling to him from across a shallow river—where the water runs to the sea. He can't hear the young woman and turns to rejoin his group. The symbolism is unmistakable: she embodies all that is good (as a Mother Mary) with his group representing the opposite. What I wanted to do was have my characters talk to that last scene and point to the "river" that separates them, whether that be the middle of America or the table they sit at. The turning point comes when they get up from the table and are able to remove, at least momentarily, the distance between them.

I wrote a decent rough and then set about revising it. I went through probably seven revisions, trying to tighten it up each time. My focus was on getting rid of extraneous, fancy lines. A week or two prior, I had attempted to watch Kevin Smith's 1994 independent feature *Clerks*, and was pretty disappointed. What bothered me the most was the dialogue. It was so loaded with "razor-sharp wit" that the lines became unbelievable and leaden—definitely on the fancy side, and really trying hard to impress. As I wrote and revised, I was very much aware that many of my lines were similar in their need to impress. So though some of those lines were my favorites, or what I considered most impressive or clever, I cut them. I recognize that this is the same process I use when revising and tightening my design work: I strive to get rid of the vacant stuff—those elements that are perhaps beautiful but add nothing to the message, story, or theme.

Despite my best efforts, some of the fancy stuff slipped through, but I was able to catch much of it later during rehearsal.

Working with the Actors

Prior to this short film, I had no real experience working with actors. So when we all got together for our first and only rehearsal—we had limited time, so we only had a single rehearsal—I really didn't know what to do. At first, I just sat back, watching and listening as the actors read through the script. It's thrilling to hear good actors reading lines you wrote, but after a few reads it becomes apparent which lines work and which don't. It also becomes apparent whether the actors are right for the parts and if there's any chemistry between them. It was either luck or just a reflection of the level of talent in New York City, but both actors, Allison Paige and Chris Trunell, were good from the start and it was clear they had chemistry. One idea I had early on, and luckily didn't act on, was to cast a friend in one of the roles. What dissuaded me was something I remembered reading in an interview with the great director Billy Wilder: "Use an actor, always use an actor, if you have a scene in a taxi cab get an actor to play the driver, even if you don't see the driver, get an actor."

As we worked through the script, I became a more active director. From the beginning, I specified to the actors that I wasn't interested in ad-libs, though I was always looking for ways to modify the lines to better suit their styles. I listened for lines that didn't work and either changed them or cut them on the spot.

With design I always demand that every element in the composition be justified in service of the larger message or theme. Once again, I drew from this experience when directing the actors. I would ask myself why each line was important and what was going on underneath it, questioning how it worked in service of the film's story and theme. In doing so, I was able to direct the actors more specifically and communicate what kind of performance I was looking for.

Sometimes I would lose my patience and actually try to act out the line myself. If Chris was saying the line too loosely, or missing the inflections I had in mind, I'd step in and say, "Hey Chris, say it like this...." For the most part, this turned out to be counterproductive, as the actor would then be concentrating on saying that one line in a certain way instead of staying in character. It reminded me of one of my biggest faults as a creative director: I sometimes stop creative directing and request that the designer hand over his or her work in progress so I can "finish it up." What worked better with the actors was simply talking to them about the characters: what they're thinking, what they struggle with, what they desire, and what they want from the other character.

For example, I instructed the actors to lean in across the table towards each other as if they want to touch each other, and explained that in fact they do, but neither is ready to "cross" the space between them. They're still drawn to each other and looking for a way to act on it, but old, unresolved issues—his decision to leave and move to New York, hers to stay in San Francisco—keep getting in the way. The characters' desires fuel everything. For Chris's character, he's a little giddy at having his old flame back in his sights, but he's also uncomfortable about it, acting nervous and jumpy. He's having a difficult transition and she represents what he misses and desires—comfort, affection, and connection. Allison's character is also conflicted. Though she, too, misses their connection, she accepts that he's left; on the other hand, she's a bit resentful and is wondering why she wasn't enough to make him stay. By communicating all of this to the actors, I was able to stop trying to control so much, and instead just direct them. In fact, I became much more open to the actors' reads of the characters' motivations and we sometimes became involved in a collaborative discussion, working our way towards a clearer understanding and approach.

The Shoot

This shoot was different for me because I didn't actually shoot it. I wisely turned that over to Ben Wolf, who along with his wife, Nara Garber, run a production company called Topiary Productions. For this film, they lit, shot, and recorded audio. We shot the spot in my New York apartment, starting at 8:30 at night and wrapping by 2 in the morning. Since Ben was responsible for the shoot, I will turn this section over to him.

When Hillman approached me to photograph his short, I eagerly agreed. Not only did I enjoy the script (having a bicoastal history myself), but I'd get a chance to work with Hillman, who I suspected would be an excellent collaborator.

I was also thrilled when Hillman agreed to cast my actor friend Chris Trunell, who I knew would excel in this demanding roll. When an entire short is set in a single location, the audience is focused on the acting, so it's got to be good.

The contained nature of this project—both in terms of locations and rehearsal/shooting time—presented challenges familiar to any low-budget filmmaker; namely, how to execute a script given extremely limited resources. I had a few possible approaches in mind, but I held off on coming up with a plan until I attended the rehearsal.

Like Hillman, I try to approach every project with a minimum of preconceptions, and let the shooting style develop organically through collaboration with the cast and director. That isn't to say there isn't a detailed game plan worked out by the time the shoot happens—but this plan has evolved through the rehearsal process, rather than being completely mapped out beforehand.

Since DV cameras are so accessible, it's usually no trouble at all to have one present at the rehearsals, and this presents a great opportunity to test different compositions, camera moves, and lighting treatments. Though I had initially imagined employing some elaborate camera moves to increase the visual interest of the scene, it quickly became clear to me that this is really a very intimate piece, and would be better served by straightforward hand-held camerawork.

Many people associate a hand-held camera with shaky home movies, and think that you should only use one when you lack a good tripod. But I believe this technique can yield great dramatic and aesthetic results when done well (which is not easy!). When a camera is "locked down," it is critical that actors precisely hit predetermined marks, and the results often look robotic. Only a hand-held camera can accommodate the spontaneous, small, natural movements that real people (and actors acting naturally) make all the time.

We used Hillman's Panasonic DVX100, and together arrived at several camera settings. For a more cinematic effect, we'd shoot in 16 x 9 widescreen at 24 frames per second. We'd mostly shoot at the telephoto end of the zoom, which generally produces more flattering close-ups. And we'd also shoot our singles "dirty"— meaning that, in the close-ups, we'd see some of the shoulder of the other person in the foreground.

When it came to lighting, we strove to keep it simple by supplementing and controlling the existing light. Gaffer Sanjay Singh relied primarily on a simple paper lantern as a key light to give a soft, flattering glow to the characters, which was consistent with the intimate night mood. We also used a scrimmed-down 200-watt Pepper (a small tungsten light) to provide a subtle backlight, separating the characters from their background. Finally, we dimmed down the practicals (lamps appearing in the scene) so that they wouldn't blow out the shot.

My wife and filmmaking partner, Nara Garber, handled the sound. She relied exclusively on a high-end boom-mounted cardioid (semidirectional) mic. Because it was fairly easy to boom this simple scene, Nara was also able to monitor and control audio levels through a small location mixer, hung from her shoulder and wired between the camera and mic.

The Edit

I had no idea how to approach the edit, never having cut a narrative film before. In fact, I just let the project sit for three or four days. When I did sit down to start the edit, going through all of the takes quickly overwhelmed me. Though I took detailed notes both in Final Cut Pro and in a notebook during the log-and-capture process, the notes weren't helping me to really organize the material or to find a rhythm. I just wasn't used to so many options. For each line spoken by the actors, there were five or six shots. Trying to determine which I should use—close-up, mid-shot, speaker, reaction, and so on—was difficult and confusing.

I sat with it for a while, finally deciding to deconstruct the entire script, line by line, in individual sequences. In other words, I'd go through each line and build a rough cut of just that line. I did this out of a kind of desperation just as a way to get started. But as I progressed I found that doing this both familiarized me with each take of each line as well as gave me quick, organized access to all of the takes.

For example, the film starts with Chris saying, "*8 1/2* plays tomorrow, if you're interested." I assembled a sequence with all six takes of that line: two mid-shots, two close-ups, and two reaction shots (where the camera is on Allison, shot from over Chris's shoulder). I then went through the film and did this for each line, ending up with close to fifty sequences. It was incredibly time consuming but, in a way, it may have saved me time in the end. By assembling each sequence like this, I was able to immerse myself deeply in the footage of the entire film and get into a rhythm with the edit. It made identifying the

best take quick and easy: I'd just play the sequence and watch all
five or six takes back to back. Additionally, if I decided to change
a shot in the main edit—say, use a mid-shot of Allison instead of a
close-up—I could easily locate and compare the shots.

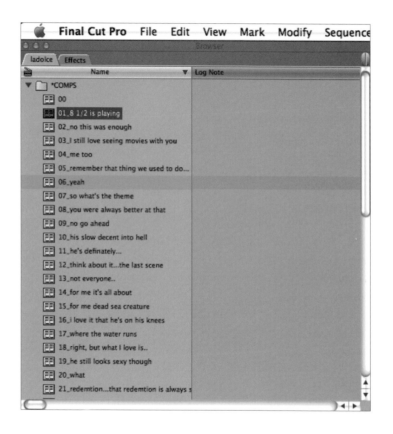

Once I had broken the script down into the individual sequences, I set about building the main edit. Years ago, when I was
designing Flash motion spots, I would find inspiration by going to
apple.com/quicktime and perusing the movie trailers there until
I found one that approximated the mood I had in mind for whatever spot I was working on. It worked well because I was able to

mimic some of the moves, transitions, and moods in the trailers. So before I started the edit with "La Dolce Vita," which is what I called my short film, I hit the trailers page at Apple and found a beautiful trailer for a movie called *YES*. It was wonderfully edited— not too fast, but not too revealing either. It gave you a glimpse into the story, which was based on a love triangle; more important than that, though, it revealed strong themes of desire, faith, and choice. During the edit, I would watch it from time to time, trying to cop a bit of the feel of the spot.

The main challenge of the edit was to keep the piece moving. The two characters are seated at the table for much of the short, so I wanted to have a lot of quick edits. I had visualized using mid-shots as a way to communicate those times when the characters are distant or pushing each other away, and coming back to the close-ups when they are connecting again. I wanted to use the selection of shots as a way to reinforce the emotion of the scene. Unfortunately, I couldn't use the mid-shot of Chris because it was framed in such a way as to make him look tiny. So I had to stay in close-up throughout the entire table scene. Nevertheless, this was a valuable lesson; next time I will think more about the camera: where it's positioned and how that affects the emotion of the scene. Additionally, this is where I learned to write no more than 1–2 pages of dialogue per scene, keeping the action moving and using that action to further reinforce the theme as well as the characters' emotions and desires.

Whenever I get a piece into a decent rough edit I post it online and share it with a few of my designer and film friends, asking for feedback. In the case of "La Dolce Vita" I sent it around to about seven or eight people. One of them, the music video director Adam Levite (associatesinscience.com), wrote back that he liked it but wanted to see more of the character's body language during the table scene. He was responding both to the fact that I couldn't use the mid-shot of Chris and that I left the characters at the table too long. Both are mistakes that I don't intend on repeating.

Sound

As an equal partner to the image in film, sound is extremely important. And so easy to screw up. I've botched the sound many times
on different projects, so when Ben suggested we bring in Nara
as sound recordist I didn't hesitate. She captured very clean and
consistent sound throughout the shoot; however, there are times
in the edit when I needed to use a couple seconds of image without the accompanying audio.

For example, I wanted to use a shot of Allison wandering
around the living room, but Chris could be heard reciting the end
of his line off camera from the kitchen. What I needed to do was
take Chris's line out and replace it with "room sound": the sound
of the room with no one talking or moving. You'd be surprised at
how much sound there is in a "quiet" room, and it's crucial to be
able to use this room sound to patch your audio track together.
Fortunately, as a professional Nara knew to go from room to room
in the apartment and capture sixty seconds of room sound, just in
case this situation presented itself.

As for scoring, in my documentaries I always use music to accompany the footage. This is especially the case in the designer series (see "My Favorite Designers"), where I often have a montage of the designer's work set to music. The fact that I love music so much just adds to the pleasure of making movies, and a good score can, in my opinion, make or break a movie.

Not long ago I was doing some site design for Fox Searchlight Pictures and was treated to a private screening of the movie *Kinsey* before they added the score. I left the screening less than impressed, with a feeling that the film wasn't completely working. A few months later I saw the finished film and couldn't believe the difference that the music made. It was the same film, but the score had completed it. And when I think of two recent films that are among my favorites—P.T. Anderson's *Magnolia* and Wes Anderson's *The Royal Tenenbaums*—I think about how much I enjoy the films *and* the scores. On the other hand, I saw a film this year called *Crash* and the music that was chosen for the final ten or twelve minutes basically ruined the movie for me. The point is that the scoring of a film offers an amazing opportunity to impact the overall quality of the film, and shouldn't be taken lightly.

For "La Dolce Vita," I ended up using four songs, one from the band Death Cab for Cutie, one from The Jesus and Mary Chain, and two from Sufjan Stevens. I love using tracks from bands or performers I like, but there are a couple of problems. One is that technically you need to obtain permission to use someone's music. This almost always involves music-licensing lawyers and money. The second problem is that it's very easy to overuse the music because you like it so much. Especially with a project like this one; I was unsure of the script and didn't feel confident enough to let long stretches of dialogue go without some sort of musical accompaniment. What happened was that the music started to detract from the film, coming and going with no real attachment to the emotions of a particular scene.

Scoring "La Dolce Vita" really opened my eyes to the difficulty of this aspect of filmmaking. Immediately after I finished my imperfect but acceptable final edit, I made a note to interview some sound designers for my next film—whatever that may be. Though I am a huge proponent of the DIY philosophy, I am aware of how much a talented specialist can bring to a project. I also began to really listen to movies. Now when I watch a movie, I find myself not only trying to figure out the camera setup in a scene but also listening to the way the sound designer adds to the emotion of that scene with music—using songs, melodies, or orchestral swells.

Which brings me back to the DIY philosophy. I have to go through a process like this, scoring a film myself, in order to recognize what music to choose or even when music is inappropriate for the scene.

In Sum

This short is about two people talking about a film. It is literally a film about film, shot for nothing in my apartment with volunteer actors. We used one camera, three six-dollar DV tapes, a few lights, and a single mic. It's flawed and imperfect, maybe a little long on the dialogue in places, but that's okay. If nothing else, it's encouraged me to write another script and try again, moving closer to the place I want to be as a filmmaker.

I did this by creating a framework of parameters and expectations; the parameters were that I shoot a short film, with limited locations and characters and with a script based on one of my favorite films. This made filming this short manageable for me. By creating a set of parameters I created problems that needed to be solved. As a designer I am used to this; it made working through a script possible because I knew ahead of time that there wouldn't be more than three characters, no more than one location, and the script would borrow thematically from a favorite film.

In my design work, I always say that limitations lead to creativity—that the fact that your client insists on blue and Arial, or that a file size for a Web page be under 100k, will actually lead to greater creativity than if you had been given a blank slate with no limitations or parameters. And it worked the same here.

As far as my expectations, they were high but not unrealistically high. I mentioned some of my favorite filmmakers earlier, and it would have been very easy for me to have talked myself out of this project simply because it would be nowhere near the level set by these artists. But by not swinging for the fences I was able to build up confidence, base hit by base hit (apologies for the lame analogy).

I've since decided to make this film the first in a series of "films about films," where I write and shoot short scripts that are somehow influenced or based on my favorite films. It's not unlike the designer series in its motivation for me; I want to learn through doing and at the same time produce work that is good enough to attract future film work.

CONCLUSION

YOU KNOW HOW YOU'RE

ALWAYS TRYIN' TO GET

THINGS TO COME OUT PERFECT

IN ART, BECAUSE IT'S REAL

DIFFICULT IN LIFE.

—WOODY ALLEN, *ANNIE HALL* (1977)

LIFE IS "TRYING THINGS TO SEE IF THEY WORK."

—RAY BRADBURY

I write a lot about the importance of reinventing oneself as an artist. It's the path I've followed, and it's part of the deal when you're a New Media designer. Some artists spend a lifetime working in the same medium, and I'm grateful to them for showing how expansive, how elastic, how limitless a single medium can be. But that hasn't been my path so far. As a kid I wanted to be a writer, and I studied writing and film in college. Then I was in a rock band. Then I did some poster design on the side, which led fortuitously to the Web in the mid-1990s. But even after I'd made a name for myself in Web design, I knew I hadn't reached the endpoint.

I started to think about this book in early 2003, and the first proposal I presented to my publishers was very different from the book you've just read. At that time I was physically and emotionally burned out. I walked around Manhattan like a robot and approached my work the same way—a huge change from the exuberance I'd felt since founding my company in 1998. Between '98 and 2001 things were great—as a New Yorker, as a Web designer, and as the owner of my own firm. Work was plentiful, money was good, and spirits were high all around.

But by 2003 things were different. As I mention in "The Visitors," the whole city was still reeling from the one-two punch of 9/11 and the ensuing economic downturn—and so was I. So following that old adage, "Write what you know," I proposed a book. It was basically about being a burned-out artist and offering a few half-baked ideas on how to pull yourself out of a creative rut. But clearly I wasn't in a position to give advice at that time. After all, I wasn't doing so great myself.

I remember my editor giving me very gentle feedback on the proposal, which was really more like some unsolicited advice: "Are you sure you want to write about this?" she asked. "Maybe a therapist would be better...."

So I batted around a few different ideas for the book over the course of a year or so, trying to find a direction and a subject that would be both exciting to write about and, hopefully, valuable to the reader. I must have drafted a dozen outlines, brainstormed as many titles, and even started writing three or four times. None of them clicked, and each time that I found myself in another dead-end, my malaise grew deeper.

Meanwhile I started shooting The Visitors portrait series, which lead to the designer series, and so on. What came next was something I hadn't intended: I not only stumbled upon the topic of this book, I also began to pull myself out of the doldrums I'd been stuck in for years.

A lifelong *cineaste*, I've always wanted to make films. This is why I loved Flash from the beginning: it allowed me to work in motion. But it never quite satisfied my desire to work with the moving image. And even back then, I had no doubt that online video was on the horizon. I was convinced—as I am now—that video on the Web would soon become the primary online medium, and that I could carve out new opportunities for myself creating films for the Web.

But that's business. Mostly, I love film because I love stories. As I mention earlier in the book, I am a firm believer in what I call "metaphorical thinking"—finding greater meaning in seemingly everyday events. I believe we can sometimes find our way in life by simply paying attention to the details that comprise a given day: a book you happen upon by chance, something you see, or a random encounter with a friend or stranger. So to wrap things up, I'll share one more story with you, about a trip I made just as this book was nearing completion.

In June 2005 the design firm Pentagram invited me to film their annual partners meeting at a small villa on the southeastern coast of Italy, just south of Bari. Compared to Rome and Florence, Bari is not a major tourist spot, but its location along the Adriatic Sea makes it one of the most beautiful and quintessentially Italian places in the country. The villa was no exception.

Pentagram is a 34-year-old design partnership with offices in London, New York, Austin, San Francisco, and Berlin. The collective is responsible for some of the best work out there, and some of their partners are design heroes of mine. Just being around this very creative and accomplished group was exciting enough, but actually being flown to Italy to film them was a true honor.

I brought along one of my oldest friends, photographer Gary Matoso, to take still shots of the twenty partners as they interacted with each other, showed each other their work, and held meetings. Meanwhile, I interviewed and filmed each partner over the five-day stay and came away with some great footage.

At one point between interviews, I walked out onto the courtyard of the villa and sat down at a café table. I ordered a glass of wine from the waiter, and another for Gary as he approached. Gary sat down, and when the wine arrived I remember taking a sip and saying to him, "This isn't so bad." Gary laughed and quickly replied, "What are you talking about? This is @#x$&%* great!"

It's a moment I hope to never forget, because it serves to remind me that following your heart can lead you to some wonderful places, and also that it takes courage to follow your heart. As Stefan Sagmeister puts it:

As I write this, I am about a third of the way into editing the six hours of footage I shot in Italy. I have no idea what I'll end up with, and I'm often discouraged by how slowly it's going. I'm also aware that I'm making a fraction of what I'd make for a Web design job. And in one week I will film the second short in the "Films on Films" series that I started with the short "La Dolce Vita," which I shot for this book and wrote about in the final chapter.

Not only do I make no money with these projects, I actually end up losing money by paying the actors and crew. I'm over 40 now, with a mortgage and a family. I'm turning down paying Web design jobs to shoot these short films, and however real the risks may be, I also know that I'm doing something I have to do. Because when I'm not up in the middle of the night calculating my expenses, I feel good. I'm thinking about scripts and camera angles and what I need to learn about lighting. Or I'm thinking about the three minutes of perfect filmmaking I noticed in an average film my wife and I watched earlier, where the art direction was perfect, the script tight, the lighting sublime, and the actors amazing.

And that's what this book is all about: the celebration of film, and the exhilaration of doing it yourself.

Looking over this book I realize that it's also about the power of making art. It's about moving beyond the depression and ennui that had overcome me just a few years ago to find myself on location, camera in hand, counting my blessings to be privileged with creativity. It's about doing what you love, or at least giving it a good shot. And it's about reading the writing on the wall: good, cheap DV cameras plus good, cheap DV editing software plus the expanding bandwidth of the Web equals something undeniable and approaching fast.

In the end, it's an investment: I'm investing in my passion, in what I believe is the future of Web design. And by writing this book, I have faith that others can benefit from what I've learned along the way. I hope it has been helpful to you.

THE CONVERSATIONS WERE ABOUT IDEAS. NO ONE WAS TALKING ABOUT MONEY.

—JIM JARMUSCH

THE THING I LOVE MOST, AS THE

YEARS GO BY, IS WORKING

ON PROJECTS WHERE I DON'T

KNOW WHAT I'M DOING.

—PAULA SCHER, ON DESIGN

APPENDIX :
WHY FLASH VIDEO?

BY JENS LOEFFLER

Now, more than ever, Macromedia Flash represents the future in motion Web design. For years, Flash has been the *de facto* standard for animation and interactivity on the Web. It has a huge development community and an even larger user-base—but that's old news. The *new* news is Flash Video, a recent addition from Macromedia that once again secures Flash's position at the vanguard of New Media design. And its relevance to this book could not be greater: Flash Video also creates unprecedented opportunities for anyone making short films for the Web.

With Flash Video, developers can seamlessly integrate video into their Web site designs, add layers over the video itself, control the video's playback, and even add interactive hotspots. Flash Video also supports video streaming; and with the help of the Flash Communication Server MX, complex video conferencing and collaboration applications can be built. And all of this can be played with the Flash Player—with no additional software for the end-user—and can be built with the Flash authoring tool.

Every Flash Player (versions 6 and higher) features the Sorenson Spark video codec, which is based on the H263 video specification and is similar to the QuickTime Sorenson Video 3 codec. It enables high-quality video playback on all platforms—whether Windows, Mac, or even Linux. This flexibility makes the Flash Player a popular choice among developers and clients alike.

Flash Video vs. The Other Guys

Other current Web video formats include Apple's QuickTime, Real Network's Real Media, and Microsoft Windows' Media technology. All well-known, well-respected platforms. And this raises the question: Is Flash Video better than the rest? Some basic facts and statistics provide a clear answer to this question.

According to an independent, third-party census, Flash Player 6 (the first video-enabled version of the player) is currently installed on more than 96% of all notebook and desktop computers. This means that almost every computer out there can play Flash Video without additional downloads or installations. You do, however, have to download QuickTime and Real Media—and end-users might not be able or don't want to download those players. Microsoft, on the other hand, has bundled its Windows Media Player with all Windows operating systems since the release of Windows 98, but it still doesn't have the cross-platform penetration of the Flash Player. And if you use a Mac, you have to download the Windows Player. Flash is most likely already there.

User experience and usability are also key factors. The Flash Player does not feature any predefined video controls, nor does it take long to buffer a video clip. Because the player is integrated into the Flash software, it gives the designer enough options to fit the video into the design of any Web site and allows for almost instant playback. This raises the potential disadvantage of not having standard video controls. Without a "stand alone" player, but rather a "custom" software player, users who need basic controls—such as *play*, *stop*, *pause*, etc.—must either build their own players using the Flash authoring tool, use Macromedia's Media Components, or use an off-the-shelf, third-party Flash player.

To clarify, I will demonstrate how to publish your Web video in a few simple steps. My goal here is to help you use Flash Video without requiring the authoring software mentioned above, which I believe only complicates your task and consumes valuable time. I will also include the source file for this demonstration as a link, allowing you to modify your own player at will.

How I Use Flash Video

Say you've just edited a video clip using your favorite editing software. (I use Final Cut Pro, also known as FCP, but the process I provide below is not limited to that software.) Now you want to encode it into a Flash Video format, and then post your spot to the Web. You can do it in just three steps:

1. Encode the source video to Flash.
2. Build or use a Flash file that plays your video.
3. Upload your files to a Web server or to a Flash Communication Server.

Step One: Encoding

Basically, encoding in Flash is the conversion and compression of a video file into the Flash Video format. Note the difference here between the FLV and SWF formats. An SWF file is the vector-based format for the Flash Player, while the FLV format defines a Flash Video file that can be downloaded from a Web server or streamed from a Flash Communication Server. You cannot play an FLV file on its own; you need to have an SWF that points to an FLV file, which will play inside the Flash player.

To begin encoding you need to have Flash Video encoding software. For example, Flash MX Professional 2004 comes with the Flash Video Exporter, which is a plug-in for QuickTime that enables you to export FLV from most QuickTime-enabled video software. You can also download the Flash Video Updater from Macromedia's Web site; that will add functionality to your video editing software to allow you to export to Flash Video. There are also some third-party vendors offering Flash Video-encoding products, namely Sorenson Squeeze from Sorenson Media and Flix from ON2 Technologies, but I'm going to focus on the Macromedia Video Exporter because it is already bundled with Flash MX Professional 2004. If you decide to work with third-party software, simply transfer the settings and process I describe here to fit your own application.

Let's assume your project was edited with FCP and is ready to export to Flash. First you should be aware of all "non-square formats." DV footage is in a non-square pixel format, while the Web uses square pixels. The difference between them is simple: Broadcast technology, such as that used by analog TV screens, uses a unique pixel format that is taller than the square pixels used on computer screens, which means you can fit more pixels horizontally on the screen with the same aspect ratio. So if you do not convert non-square footage to fit a square pixel-screening platform, you'll see horizontally stretched video; for instance, in playback a golf ball will look like an egg.

When you export your video in the square pixel format, your editing software will automatically adjust the screen size and display the video with the right dimensions. If your video editing software doesn't support square video export, changing the aspect ratio to 4:3 should do the job. In Final Cut Pro, select QuickTime Conversion as the export option and choose "Movie to Macromedia Flash Video (FLV)" in the export settings.

The Options button will lead you to a detailed settings menu. Note that the encoding quality is closely related to the data-rate and available bandwidth.

Common encoding settings are:

Setting	Video Data-rate	Audio Data-rate	Frame-rate	Size
Broadband high quality	382 kbits/s	128 kbits/s (Stereo)	15 fps	320 x 240
Broadband standard	204 kbits/s	96 kbits/s (Stereo)	15 fps	320 x 240
Modem/ Dial-up	24 kbits/s	16 kbits/s (Mono)	8 fps	160 x 120

Although 29.97 fps is the standard frame-rate for the NTSC format, it is not recommended to use this frame-rate if your target audience is using Macs, because the speed of the Flash Player plug-in on the Macintosh is a bit slower than the Windows version and you might drop some frames during the playback. This will most likely change in future Flash Player versions, but for now it is worth noting.

Other recommendations are:

Encoding Method: Best (2 Pass)   2-pass encoding is available in Flash Video Encoder versions 1.1 and higher. 2-pass increases video quality by using an additional pass that analyzes your footage to maximize its output quality. Always use 2-pass encoding unless you are in a rush and need to complete the encoding process quickly.

Keyframes: Automatic   In short, a high number of keyframes is better for fast-paced video, while fewer keyframes are good for video with long scenes and little movement. Setting keyframes on automatic will result in reliably high quality for whatever you shoot.

Deinterlacing: None (with our recommended size settings)
Video recorded with broadcast video cameras is stored in an interlaced format. A DV camera normally records 59.94 half-frames (interlaced) instead of 29.97 full frames (progressive). A half-frame stores only every other vertical line. The first half-frame contains all the odd lines, the second half contains all the even lines, the third frame contains all odd lines again, and so on. Every half-frame has a short time delay in between, meaning that if you merge two half-frames into a full frame (which is used in the computer world), you'll see interlaced artifacts.

Interlaced video (broadcast television)

odd lines   even lines

Progressive Scan (computer screen)

all lines (even + odd)

Interlaced artifacts

$$\frac{1}{29.97} \text{ second}$$

The Flash Video Exporter offers a simple solution. It can use all upper (odd) or all lower (even) fields for encoding. This may reduce the resolution of your image, but you won't have interlaced artifacts. Smarter deinterlacing algorithms merge the two half-frames into a full frame without losing so much information, but the current video exporting tool unfortunately does not support this feature. This might change in forthcoming versions.

Since we're using a 320 x 240-pixel window size as our video format, the video size is reduced by 50%, freeing us from the need to deinterlace the footage since every second line will automatically be deleted.

To summarize:

Video size	Movement in the video	Interlace settings
Up to 320 x 240	Doesn't matter	None
> 320 x 240	Slow	None
> 320 x 240	Normal and fast	Even or odd

Et voila, you now have your well-encoded FLV Flash Video file.

Step Two: Create or Use an Existing Flash Video Player

With your encoded FLV video file ready to go, your next step is to create the Flash Video player. The Flash MX 2004 authoring environment can assist in building a player from scratch. However, this can be a challenging process if you are a novice to Flash authoring. If this describes you, or if you often work under tight deadlines, I suspect you will appreciate my approach. Personally, I don't like spending time in unknown territory, especially when I'm close to deadline. After all, I just want to see video on my Web project—and figuring out how to do it shouldn't take up any more time than necessary.

Flash MX Professional 2004 offers a feature called Media Components, a sophisticated set of Flash components that you can place on your Flash stage, fill out the component parameters, and use to play your video file. Of course you can also buy or download third-party video players, which might better serve your needs and look better on your Web site, or build your own player.

For designers who don't own Flash MX 2004 software, or those who have little experience using such an authoring tool, all this may seem rather daunting. Fortunately, the Flash Video player featured here can be easily configured via HTML. No need for Flash MX 2004 experience; just specify the video file in the HTML, save the file, upload it to your site, and start playing video!

You can download the player here:
http://www.flashstreamworks.com/hillmancurtisbook/
movieplayer.zip

Let's get started. Open your HTML editor of choice (Macromedia Dreamweaver, Adobe GoLive, Macromedia Homesite, etc.) and edit the object tag of the index.html file:

```
<object classid="clsid:d27cdb6e-ae6d-11cf-96b8-444553540000"
codebase="http://fpdownload.macromedia.com/pub/shockwave/cabs/
flash/swflash.cab#version=7,0,0,0" width="400" height="315"
id="movieplayer" align="middle">
<param name="allowScriptAccess" value="sameDomain" />
<param name="movie" value="movieplayer.swf" />
<param name="quality" value="high" />
<param name="bgcolor" value="#FFFFFF" />
<param NAME=FlashVars VALUE="vidpath=reel.flv">
<embed src="movieplayer.swf" FlashVars="vidpath=reel.flv"
quality="high" bgcolor="#FFFFFF" width="400" height="315"
name="movieplayer" align="middle" allowScriptAccess="sameDomain"
type="application/x-shockwave-flash" pluginspage="http://www.
macromedia.com/go/getflashplayer" />
</object>
```

Place your FLV file in the same folder in which the HTML page is located. Modify the red highlighted value, save the file, open it in a browser, and play back the video. What just happened: a Flash variable name and value with the FlashVars parameter tag just passed to the Flash Movie. The player will now use the value to locate the video and start playback.

Seem easy? Unfortunately, it's not always that simple. For example, let's say you want to show a clip in the Flash Video format to a large audience. First, you must take into consideration the amount of bandwidth you have at your disposal, and the traffic requirements of your spot. Make sure your provider has the capacity to handle large volumes of data transfer and simultaneous viewers. In addition, consider using Streaming instead of Progressive Download for playback. Progressive Download is a method of placing the FLV file on a Web server and letting viewers download the file to their computers. In this example we are using the Progressive Download method, which also allows you to play the video while it's downloading. If you have a fast Internet connection the file will begin playing almost immediately. The downside is that the file will be stored in the browser cache of the viewer's hard drive. If you and/or your client wish to prevent that, use streaming technology. By streaming Flash Video files you also optimize the way video is delivered on the Web. This method requires a special server—in our case the Flash Communication Server MX, also known as FlashCom, or Macromedia's FVSS (Flash Video Streaming Services).

How does this technology work? The streaming server sends small parts of the video to the Flash Player, which plays it back after an optional short buffering time. The file won't be downloaded to the user's machine. Plus, the Flash Player can control which parts it wants to receive next. Streaming also allows you to play long video clips without overloading the browser cache with data.

Here is a quick overview of which methods work best for specific projects:

Task	Use
I want to play a video clip that is 5 minutes or less	Progressive
I want to play a video clip that is longer than 5 minutes	Streaming
I need copyright protection	Streaming
It's okay that the user can download the video	Progressive
I want to jump to different parts of the video, and don't want to wait until this part is downloaded	Streaming
I work for a client with a high security network and I'm not sure if he allows more than just Web site traffic or has a strict firewall	Progressive

The last point I mention in the table is targeting business decision makers and technologists. Flash Video streaming uses the propriety RTMP protocol, which some firewalls or proxy servers block. Find more information about Flash Video and playback over firewalls here: http://www.macromedia.com/cfusion/knowl edgebase/index.cfm?id=tn_16466.

To address the problem of firewalls blocking the RTMP protocol Macromedia developed what it calls "HTTP tunneling." This means that the RTMP data is wrapped into standardized HTTP traffic and increases the compatibility with firewalls.

Macromedia also partnered with a few Internet Service Providers to promote the new Flash Video Service—a system to deliver video files over a robust content delivery network. For more information on how to use Flash Video streaming, visit the site of the first Flash Video Service Provider—Vital Stream (http://www.vitalstream.com)—or read this article describing the use of Flash Video with the Flash Communication Server: http://www.flashstreamworks.com/tutorials/101stream1.php

Building your own Flash Video player   If you are an experienced Flash developer and are asked to use Flash Video in an existing design, you can build your own player. Below I offer simple instructions for designing a basic player without media controls.

Requirements: Flash MX 2004 or higher and basic Flash skills. (This example will not use any external components.)

1. Open Flash and create a new Flash Movie.
2. Create a new Flash Video object in the library.
3. Place this Video object on the stage.
4. Resize it to 320 x 240.
5. In the Property inspector, give the object the name "video-area".
6. Place a Flash Video file into the folder where the SWF file will be published and name it "video.flv".
7. Place this code into the first frame of the timeline:

```
// streaming an FLV through a local video object


// provides mechanism for playing external FLVs
var video_nc = new NetConnection();

// open local connection
video_nc.connect(null);

// we've established a connection; this controls the stream
var video_ns = new NetStream(video_nc);

// can perform error checking
video_nc.onStatus = function(infoObject) {
   if (infoObject.code == "NetConnection.Connect.Success") {
      trace("local connection successful");
   }
   if (infoObject.code == "NetConnection.Connect.Failed") {
      trace("local connection failed");
   }
};

// starts the video
video_ns.play("video.flv");

// attach the NetStream instance to the video object on the stage
videoarea.attachVideo(video_ns);

stop();
```

The script creates a connection to the local file system and plays the video file in the "videoarea" video object on the stage. In line 5 you can see how the script is connecting to "null." Null means that the file is a progressive download file and resides on a Web server. It does not require any connection to a streaming server. If you would like to connect to a streaming server, contact a Flash Communication Server provider like Vitalstream. com or Uvault.com, and specify in your script the following tag: video_nc.connect(rtmp://test.uvault.com/videos/). Or use whatever connection string your provider gives you.

By implementing this example you should be able to play your video as a Flash file. Now you can be as creative as you like. Add layers and graphics over the video, or simply let it play. You can even scale in real-time, or add alpha to it. You can treat it just as you would a regular Flash object.

Step Three: Upload Your Flash Video File

The last step is to upload the files to your Web server, or to your FlashCom hosting provider. If you are using progressive download with a regular Web server, upload the player (*.swf) and the video file (*.flv) with FTP software like Fetch (Macintosh) or SecureFX (PC) to your Web folder where your Web site's files reside. If you've decided to use streaming, most providers either provide a simple-to-use Web interface to upload the files, receive the RTMP connection string, or use their own video players to play it.

Source Download:
http://www.flashstreamworks.com/tutorials/files/
video_without_components.zip

In Sum

Creating and publishing Flash Video can be easy for some and complex for others. It is a new technology, after all. But as always, new technologies are exciting and rewarding all at the same time. Flash Video offers great benefits: it's easy to use, it offers seam-less integration with Flash-based sites and projects, it allows you to go beyond the creative borders of standard Web video, and it has a huge market share—embraced by developers and end-users alike. My clients are thrilled by its possibilities for presenting their goods and services online. What's more, the technology is still relatively young: anyone starting now can get in at the ground floor. In the end it all comes down to what Macromedia has always told us: Experience matters.

CONTRIBUTORS

David Alm

David helped me write my last book, MTIV: Process, Inspiration and Practice for the New Media Designer, *and was there with this book—especially at the start—as it's gone through its different incarnations. This book wouldn't have happened without his help.*

David Alm is a freelance journalist, editor, and teacher. He holds a master's degree from the University of Chicago, where he studied film history and theory. He has published widely on contemporary art, film, and design in magazines such as *American Artist Watercolor*, *Artbyte*, *Camerawork*, *RES*, *Silicon Alley Reporter*, *Time Out*, *SOMA*, and the *Utne Reader*. He has assisted Hillman in making several short films and documentaries. Following graduate school he taught film history at Columbia College in Chicago before moving back to New York in 2005. He lives in Brooklyn.

Ben Wolf

I trusted Ben to go through each chapter of this book to make sure the technical information was correct and current. Ben also worked as the Director of Photography and Assistant Director on two of my films.

Ben Wolf is a cinematographer, director, editor, and teacher. He and his wife/business partner Nara Garber are partners in Topiary Productions, Inc., a boutique film and video production company specializing in digital video production and post. Ben has worked as Director of Photography on numerous feature films, documentaries, television programs, and commercials. He holds an MFA in Film from Columbia University School of the Arts.

Jens Loeffler

I was lucky to find Jens to contribute his appendix on Flash Video. Jens runs a very informative blog on Flash Video (flashstreamworks.com).

Jens Loeffler has been working with Flash since 1999. He has a degree in media computer science and has received several awards for his work, including the Animago Award for Education/Interactive DVD Design and several Macromedia Web Site of the Week/Day awards for his Flash Video Web sites. Jens possesses a broad knowledge of engineering, multimedia, and design, as well as a sophisticated understanding of the Flash platform and strategy. He was involved in building one of the first Flash Communication Server Providers and he developed several FlashCom back-end solutions and applications. Currently he is working on Flash Rich Internet and Broadband/Flash Video applications.

CREDITS

Page 53
Sagmeister AIGA Detroit poster
Art Direction: Stefan Sagmeister
Photography: Tom Schierlitz
Client: AIGA Detroit
1999
27.5 x 39" (69 x 99 cm)

"For this lecture poster for the AIGA Detroit, we tried to visualize the pain that seems to accompany most of our design projects. Our intern Martin cut all the type into my skin. Yes, it did hurt real bad."

Pages 88–89
Detail of "Just Say No"
© James Victore

Page 94
"Just Say No"
© James Victore

Page 95
"The Death Penalty Mocks Justice"
© James Victore

Pages 100 and 101
Stills from the feature film *Closed Circuit*
Directed by Ben Wolf
Photographed by Milton Kam

Pages 103 and 104
Details and stills from *La Dolce Vita*. Dir: Federico Fellini. Perfs. Marcello Mastroianni, Anita Ekberg, Anouk Aimée. DVD. Distributed in the USA by Koch Lorber Films, 1960.

Page 107
"Racism and the Death Penalty"
© James Victore

Page 108
"raCism"
© James Victore

Page 111
"Celebrate Columbus"
© James Victore

Pages 118–119
Still from *MTIV* promo:
Bill Viola
The Crossing (1996)
Video/sound installation
Collection:
Edition 1, Collection of Solomon R. Guggenheim Museum, New York, gift of The Bohen Foundation
Edition 2, Collection of Pamela and Richard Kramlich, San Francisco
Edition 3, Dallas Museum of Art, Texas
Photo: Kira Perov

Pages 123, 126–127
Stills from *MTIV* promo, which feature:
Bill Viola
The Crossing (1996)

Bill Viola
The Greeting (1995)
Video/sound installation
Collection:
Edition 1, Pamela and Richard Kramlich
Edition 2, Modern Art Museum of Fort Worth, Texas
Edition 3, Kunstmuseum Basel, Switzerland
Edition 4, Ludwig Stiftung, Aachen, Germany
Edition 5, De Pont Foundation for Contemporary Art, Tilburg, The Netherlands
Artist's proof 2, Whitney Museum of American Art, New York; partial and promised gift of an anonymous donor, P.4.95
Photo: Kira Perov

Bill Viola
Stations (1994)
Video/sound installation
Edition 1, The Bohen Foundation; promised gift in honor of Richard E. Oldenburg to The Museum of Modern Art, New York
Edition 2, Museum for Contemporary Art, Zentrum fur Kunst und Medientechnologie, Karlsruhe
Photo: Charles Duprat

No Way Out Billboard by Paul Rand
The Paul Rand Collection
Yale University Library

Anatomy of a Murder. Saul Bass
The Kobal Collection

Colors #13. Tibor Kalman
© Colors Archive

Lucent Technology Center for the Performing Arts (NJPAC)
Design: Paula Scher, Rion Byrd, Pok Chow
Photo © Peter Mauss/Esto.

IKKO TANAKA. NOH PLAY "THE 5TH KANZE NOH" (1958)
© Ikko Tanaka Design Studio

Barbara Kruger
"Untitled (It's a Small World But Not If You Have To Clean It)" (1990)
Photographic silkscreen on vinyl
143 x 103 in.
The Museum of Contemporary Art, Los Angeles
Purchased with funds provided by the National Endowment for the Arts, a Federal Agency, and Douglas S. Cramer

Stills from Soulbath.com
Design: Hi-Res! London

Video stills from the film *Newport*
Design: David Hartt and Gary Breslin

Screenshots from the miniml.com site
Design: Craig Kroeger
© 2001 miniml.com

Stills from FAKTUR/A
Design: Kontruktiv.net
© Matt Anderson 2002

The lines "nobody not even the rain" and "has such small hands" are from "somewhere I have never travelled, gladly beyond," a poem by e.e. cummings. From *e. e. cummings: Complete Poems 1904–1962*, ed. George J. Firmage. (New York: Liveright Publishing, 1994).

Pages 192-193
Photo © Gary Matoso

Pages 199-204
"Having Guts Always Works Out For Me"
Design: Sagmeister Inc./Bela Borsodi
Art Direction: Stefan Sagmeister
Design: Matthias Ernstberger, Miao Wang, Stefan Sagmeister
Photo: Bela Borsodi
Client: *.copy* magazine (Austria)
2003
9 x 11.5" (230 x 295mm)

"Six newly commissioned double page spreads for the Austrian magazine *.copy*. Together they read: Having / guts / always / works out / for / me. These are dividing spaces, each opening a new chapter in the magazine. Each month the magazine commissions another studio/artist with the design."

Page 215
Images © Jens Loeffler

INDEX

A

Adobe
    Photoshop, 113, 114
    Premiere Pro, 19
    series, 92–117
Allen, Woody, 171, 194
Alm, David, 172, 222
Altman, Robert, 56
Anderson, P.T., 171, 188
Anderson, Wes, 171, 188
Apple.com, 75, 184–85
Apple "switch" ads, 155
Arena Rock Records, 153
Art and Photography, 36
art direction, 105
audio levels, 18
auto controls, 16, 96
Avedon, Richard, 29, 50
Avid, 19

B

"Basstation," 146
Bergman, Ingmar, 40
Bill Viola: The Passions, 34
black and white, 103, 109
Boyle, Danny, 14
Bradbury, Ray, 195

C

cameras
    Canon XL1, 14, 77, 126,
        148, 156
    controls for, 15–18, 64, 101
    hand-held, 180
    mics built into, 19, 80, 96

one-chip vs. three-chip, 15
    Panasonic DVX100, 15, 34,
        36, 96, 180
Canon XL1, 14, 77, 126, 148, 156
Cash, Johnny, 147
CCD chips, 15, 16
Celebration, 25
Chronicle of a Summer, 36–37
cinema verité, 36
Clerks, 173
Close, Chuck, 44
CMYK color mode, 113
codecs, 23
color correction, 48, 109
commercial artist, role of, 50, 52
compression, 22–23, 135
computers, 19
Coppola, Francis Ford, 81
Crash, 188
Creeper Lagoon, 153
Crewdson, Gregory, 50
cyc room, 156

D

Dali, Salvador, 72
Davis, John, 165
Death Cab for Cutie, 188
deinterlacing, 215–216
depth of field, 16, 100–101
designer series, 92–117
diCorcia, Philip-Lorca, 50, 127
digital video (DV)
    advantages of, 5–6, 14
    equipment for, 15–20
    film vs., 149

future of, 4, 197, 205
    process for, 21–25
directing, 44, 105, 157, 174–75
drives, external FireWire, 20

E

Eberts, Jake, 148
editing, 22, 81. See also
    individual projects
encoding, 212-216
Eno, Brian, 91
equipment, 15–20
exposure
    adjusting, 16–17
    importance of, 16

F

Fellini, Federico, 103, 105, 106,
    168–69, 171, 172
Figgis, Mike, 124, 130
"Films on Films" series, 191, 205
Final Cut Pro
    competitors to, 19
    compression utility in, 23
    MiniDV decks and, 20
    video export with, 213-214
firewalls, 219
FireWire
    drives, external, 20
    port, 15
The Five Obstructions, 60
Flash Video
    advantages of, 23–24, 210-
        211, 221
    encoding in, 212-216
    files, uploading, 221

for nonlinear storytelling, 122,
125, 128
player, existing, 216-219
player, new, 219-220
Flix, 212
FLV format, 212
focal length, 101
focusing, 16
Fox, Adam, 150, 160
Fox Searchlight Pictures, 188
Franju, Georges, 120
F-stops, 16, 101

G

gain, 17
Gap ads, 155
Garber, Nara, 176, 182, 187
Gherardi, Piero, 105
Girls Against Boys, 130-33, 136,
139, 146-50, 156, 165
Glaser, Jonathan, 146
Glaser, Milton, 93
Godard, Jean-Luc, 36, 121, 122
Goldin, Nan, 50
"Golden Porsche," 58, 60
Gondry, Michel, 146
Gottlieb, Doug, 74-75
Guzman, Luis, 124

H

headphones, 19
heart, following your, 153, 154,
165, 198
Hemingway, Ernest, 81
Herzog, Werner, 145
Hillman, Sid, 149
HTTP tunneling, 219
"Hurt," 147

I

IEEE 1394. *See* FireWire
i.Link, 15
images, converting, 113-14
interlacing, 215-216
interviewing, 78, 102
iris, 16, 101

J

Jacob's Ladder, 150, 165
Janney, Eli, 146, 156
Jarmusch, Jim, 206
The Jesus and Mary Chain, 188
Jonze, Spike, 146

K

Kaufman, Anthony, 63
keyframes, 214
Kinsey, 188
Kovalik, Ian, 148
Kubrick, Stanley, 12, 22

L

"La Dolce Vita" (Curtis), 170-91
La Dolce Vita (Fellini), 103,
105-6, 172
lavalier mics, 18-19
Leaving Las Vegas, 130
Leth, Jørgen, 60, 63, 68
Levite, Adam, 185
lighting, 39-41, 133, 180
The Limey, 124
limitations, 60, 63, 68, 190
Loeffler, Jens, 223
logging and capturing, 21-22
Lumet, Sidney, 157

Lumière, Auguste and Louis, 87
Lynch, David, 124
Lyne, Adrian, 150

M

Macromedia. *See* Flash Video;
Media Components; Video
Exporter
Magnolia, 188
Mantle, Anthony Dod, 14
Mastroianni, Marcello, 172
Matoso, Gary, 198
Media Cleaner Pro, 23
Media Components, 211, 216
microphones, 18-19, 80, 96
MiniDV decks, 20
Mogwai, 58, 60, 66, 106, 109
monitors, 20
Morris, Errol, 78
Movement Study, 58-68
MTIV promo, 125-28, 139
Mulholland Drive, 124
Müller-Brockmann, Josef, 154
music, 188-89
music videos
for Girls Against Boys,
146-50, 165
for Superdrag, 153, 155-56,
158-63, 165

N

ND filters, 17
"next step" projects, 165
Nickelback, 79-80
Nicks, Stevie, 77
NTSC monitors, 20
Nykvist, Sven, 40

O

Observance, 36

P

Paige, Allison, 174, 175, 183, 184, 187
Pam Tanowitz Dance Company, 58
Panasonic DVX100, 15, 34, 36, 96, 180
Parker, Dorothy, 81
Pentagram, 198
The Perfect Human, 60
pixels, shape of, 114, 213
post-production, 22
Premiere Pro, 19
pre-production, 21
production, 21
progressive download, 218, 221

Q

Q-Tip, 159
QuickTime
    codec for, 23
    Flash vs., 23, 24, 210-211
    Player, 22, 23
    video export and, 212

R

Rauschenberg, Robert, 33
Real Media, 22, 23, 24, 210, 211
RES, 130
research, 155
resolution, 113
RGB, 113
Robbins, Tim, 150
Rollingstone.com, 74–87, 130
Romanek, Mark, 147
room sound, 187
Rouch, Jean, 36–37

The Royal Tenenbaums, 188
RTMP protocol, 219
Ruff, Thomas, 36, 37, 50

S

Sagmeister, Stefan, 52, 92, 198
Scher, Paula, 93, 207
Schmidt, Peter, 91
scoring, 188–89
Scratch, 52
shadows, 135
shotgun mics, 18
shutter speed, 16–17
"Sine Wave," 106, 109
Singh, Sanjay, 180
60 Seconds with..., 74–87
Smith, Kevin, 173
Soderbergh, Steven, 124, 171
software, 19
Sony
    cameras, 15
    Vegas Video, 19
Sorenson
    Spark video codec, 210
    Squeeze, 23, 212
sound, 77, 79–80, 182, 187–89
speakers, 19
split screen, 131, 136, 139
"The Staggering Genius," 153
Stamp, Terence, 124
Stevens, Sufjan, 188
storytelling, nonlinear, 122–39
streaming, 218-219, 221
Struth, Thomas, 50
Sum 41, 75–85
Superdrag, 153, 155–56, 158–63, 165
SWF format, 212

T

Tanowitz, Pam, 58
tape, 112
Tenenbaum, Karen, 92
Time Code, 124, 130, 131
time code, checking, 112
Topiary Productions, 176
tripods, 41
Truffaut, Francois, 36
Trunell, Chris, 174, 175, 177, 183, 185, 187
28 Days Later, 14, 25

V

Vegas Video, 19
Victore, James, 94–100, 102, 106–12, 113–17
Video Exporter, 212
Viola, Bill, 34, 36, 37, 127
Visitors portrait series, 24, 30–52
"Vivrant Thing," 159
von Trier, Lars, 60, 63, 68

W

Weiss, Steve, 125
white balance, 17
Wilder, Billy, 174
Williams, Hype, 159
Windows Media Player, 4, 22, 23, 24, 211
Wolf, Ben, 171, 176, 187, 223

Y

YES, 185

Z

zoom, 16